SCIENCE
THROUGH
ACTIVE
READING

Earth and Physical Science

Content and Learning Strategies

Mary Ann Christison
Sharron Bassano

Addison-Wesley Publishing Company

Reading, Massachusetts • Menlo Park, California • New York
Don Mills, Ontario • Wokingham, England • Amsterdam
Bonn • Sydney • Singapore • Tokyo • Madrid • San Juan

Earth and Physical Science: Content and Learning Strategies

Executive editor: Joanne Dresner
Development editor: Debbie Sistino
Production editor: Janice L. Baillie
Text design: Joseph DePinho
Cover design: Joseph DePinho
Cover photo: Science Source/Photo Researchers
Text art: Lloyd P. Birmingham

Library of Congress Cataloging-in-Publication Data
Christison, Mary Ann.
    Earth and physical science: content and learning strategies / Mary Ann Cristison,
    Sharron Bassano.
        p.   cm. — (Science through active reading)
        ISBN 0-8013-0348-6
        1. Readers—Science.   2. English language—Textbooks for foreign
    speakers.   3. Science—Problems, exercises, etc.   I. Bassano,
    Sharron.   II. Title.   III. Series: Bassano, Sharron.   Science
    through active reading.
    PE1127.S3C54   1991
    428.6'4'0245—dc20   91-4279
                                                                      CIP

ISBN: 0-8013-0348-6

8 9 10-CRS-99 98

CONTENTS

LEARNING STRATEGIES

Using prior knowledge ☆ Working cooperatively ☆
Inferencing ☆ Self-evaluation ☆ Reading selectively

TO THE STUDENT

Earth Science and **Physical Science** study the earth and its parts. Earth science and physical science study our earth's environment. You will study six different topics in this short introduction to earth and physical science.

Meteorology is the study of weather.

Topography is the study of the surface of the earth and such things as mountains and rivers.

Oceanography is the study of the oceans and seas.

Physics and **Chemistry** study the things that make up the earth and the energy and forces inside, around, and on the earth.

Astronomy is the study of the universe—the stars, the moons, and the planets.

With this book you will learn to follow the scientific thinking process. You will do the following things:

Consult with others:	Share ideas in cooperative groups
Make hypotheses:	Guess possible answers to questions or problems
Experiment:	Try to prove your guesses were correct
Observe:	Watch and take notes on what you see
Read:	Learn new information and remember it
Classify:	Put things or ideas into groups or categories
Compare and contrast:	Discover how something is different from another or the same as another thing

Make conclusions:	Decide if your guesses were correct or if you need to change your ideas
Report:	Discuss your conclusions with the whole class

You will also have the chance to ask and answer questions in the way scientists do. Earth and physical scientists ask these kinds of questions:

★ What are the moon and stars made of?
★ What forces shape the earth?
★ How is the earth's atmosphere changing?
★ How do the earth's great oceans create weather?

This book will give you the opportunity to explore and discover many interesting ideas and facts about your world. It will give you a fine beginning in physical science.

1

METEOROLOGY

WEATHER AND CLIMATE: WHAT IS THE DIFFERENCE?

INTRODUCTION

Everyone likes to talk about the **weather**. The weather starts many conversations. People are always interested in what the weather will be tomorrow. "Do I need my umbrella?" "Can we have our baseball game?" "Should I take my jacket?" "Will it be a good day for a hike in the mountains?" We look for answers to these questions in the weather report on TV. We read weather charts in the newspaper. We listen to the weather report on the radio. Then we plan our day.

In this chapter, you will learn what makes the weather. You will learn the difference between weather and **climate**, and you will study different climates in different parts of the world.

1

WHAT DO YOU ALREADY KNOW ABOUT WEATHER AND CLIMATE?

LEARNING STRATEGIES
☆ Using prior knowledge
☆ Working cooperatively

Read these sentences. Draw a circle around the words you do not understand. Underline the words you cannot pronounce.

Air is all around us.

The sun warms the earth.

The earth warms the air.

Wind is moving air.

When water freezes, it becomes ice.

Ice melts and becomes water.

Rain and snow come from certain types of clouds.

The North Pole and the South Pole are very cold regions.

Near the equator the climate is very hot.

Mountain weather is different from desert weather.

Sit down with a partner. Look at your book and your partner's book. Help each other understand the words that are circled. Help each other pronounce the words that are underlined.

THINK ABOUT THESE IDEAS

LEARNING STRATEGIES
☆ Interpreting data
☆ Taking notes
☆ Self-evaluation

Work in groups of three or four. Work together to answer these questions. If you are not sure about the answers, guess!

1. Look at the pictures. Read the words below. Choose the correct word for each picture.

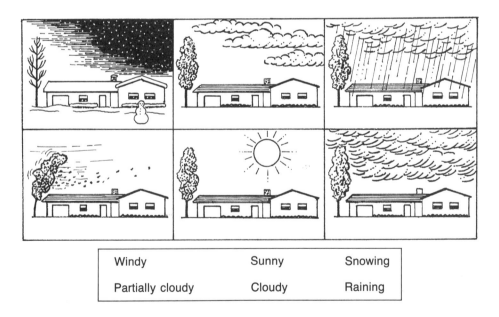

Windy	Sunny	Snowing
Partially cloudy	Cloudy	Raining

2. When we talk about the weather or the climate in different parts of the world, we have to talk about **latitudes**. Latitudes are

imaginary lines around the earth that measure the distance north or south from the **equator**. Look at the map of the world.

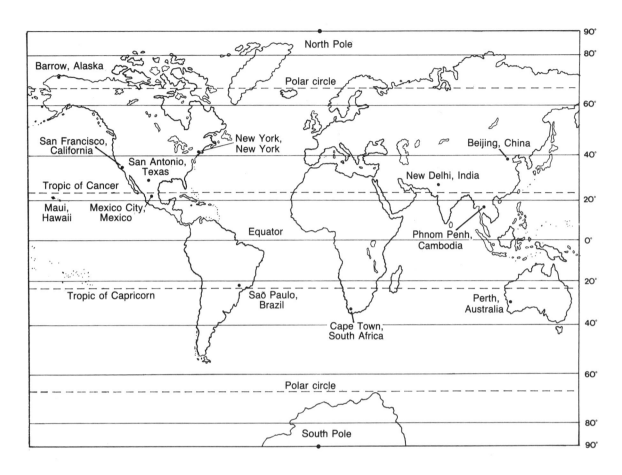

a. Find the equator. The equator is an imaginary line that goes around the earth at its widest part. The equator is 0° latitude.

b. The area north of the equator is called the **Northern Hemisphere**. The bottom half is called the **Southern Hemisphere**. Find the **Tropic of Cancer**. It is in the Northern Hemisphere at about 23½° latitude.

c. Find the **Tropic of Capricorn**. It is in the Southern Hemisphere at 23½° latitude.

d. Find the two **polar circles**. They are about 67° latitude in both the Northern and the Southern Hemispheres.

e. Find the **North Pole** and the **South Pole**. Their latitude is 90°, the exact top and bottom of the earth.

3. With your partners, find the latitudes of the following cities on the map. In your notebooks write down the latitudes and write *N* or *S* to show which hemisphere they are in—north or south.

New York, New York	Perth, Australia
New Delhi, India	Maui, Hawaii
San Antonio, Texas	San Francisco, California
Mexico City, Mexico	Saõ Paulo, Brazil
Beijing, China	Phnom Penh, Cambodia
Barrow, Alaska	Cape Town, South Africa

4. Share your ideas about these questions with your group.

   a. Sometimes when you take a shower, the mirrors and windows in the bathroom become wet. Where does the water on the glass come from?

   b. If you put an inch of water in a pot and boil it on the stove for a short time, the water will "disappear." Where does the water go?

   c. You have seen pictures of hot-air balloons. They have no motor or engine. They are controlled by hot air. A small tank of gas is under the balloon. A fire is lit. The balloon slowly fills with hot air from the flame. When the balloon is full it rises up into the air. Why?

   d. In the supermarket, you see frozen food and ice cream in a freezer case with no door on top. Why does the food stay frozen hard even when there is no door on the freezer case?

When your group finishes talking about these ideas, share your ideas with the whole class. Are your ideas different? Are they similar? After you read this chapter, look at these ideas and your answers again. Do not worry if your answers are right or wrong.

GROUP OBSERVATIONS

LEARNING STRATEGIES
☆ Inferencing
☆ Working cooperatively
☆ Self-evaluation

Materials

2 cups of dirt	1 cup of ice cubes	a tall glass
a tablespoon	2 small dishes	a pie tin

Before completing these activities make a hypothesis. A hypothesis is a guess about what you think will happen. Then see if your hypothesis is correct after you do the experiment. An experiment is an activity that checks to see if your hypothesis is correct. Read each experiment and write each hypothesis in your notebook. Then do the experiments. Work in groups.

1. Put a tablespoon of water in a small dish. Put the dish in the sun. Put a tablespoon of water in another small dish. Put this dish in a cool, shaded place. Check the dishes in about an hour. What do you think will be the difference between the two dishes after an hour? What do you think will cause the difference?

2. Fill the pie tin with loose dirt. Pour water in the tin until all the dirt is moist or a little wet. Put the dish in the sun for two days. What do you think will happen to the dirt after two days? What do you think will cause the difference in the dirt?

3. Fill a glass with ice cubes and water. Put the glass in the sun. What do you think will happen to the outside of the glass after about 10 minutes? What do you think will cause the change in the glass?

Share your answers with the whole class. After you finish reading this chapter, come back to these questions and observations and read them again. Are your answers the same?

FOCUS QUESTION

Skim the reading on pages 5, 6, and 7 to find the answer to the question below. Underline the answer in your book. Write the answer below.

■ *What is the difference between weather and climate?* ____

_____

DETAIL QUESTIONS

LEARNING STRATEGY
☆ **Reading selectively**

Read ''Weather and Climate Are Not the Same Thing'' on pages 5, 6, and 7. Find the details. Underline the answers in your book. Write the answers below. As you read, write down any words you do not understand or cannot pronounce on small slips of paper your teacher will give you. Then give these ''vocabulary tickets'' to your teacher. Do not write your name on the tickets. Your teacher and the whole class will review the words together.

1. What causes weather? _____

_____

2. What are two things that change weather? _____

_____

3. Name the five climate-makers. _____

_____

READING 1 ★

Weather and Climate Are Not the Same Thing

What is **weather**? Weather is the condition of the air, or **atmosphere**, at one time and in one particular place. Some words you know that describe weather are sunny, windy, cloudy, rainy, and stormy. Weather

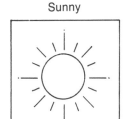

Sunny

Monday

Partially cloudy

Tuesday

Cloudy

Wednesday

Rainy

Thursday

Stormy

Friday

is not just local, however, It is worldwide. Weather in one part of the world causes changes in weather in other parts of the world. And the weather changes every day.

What causes weather? This may surprise you, but it is the sun. Energy from the sun heats the land and the oceans. Then the earth and water send heat back up into the air. Warm air is lighter than cold air. Cold air moves in under the warm air and pushes it up. Warm air rises, and cool air falls. This movement of air is called wind. The wind blows clouds around the earth. This air movement changes weather in every part of the world. Water, or **moisture**, in the air also helps to change the weather. Water rises up into the air in the form of a gas from lakes and oceans, and even from the earth. This water in the air forms fog, clouds, snow, and rain.

How is weather different from **climate**? The important difference between weather and climate is time. The weather in an area may change every day, but the climate in that area changes very little and very slowly. You know that weather is the condition of the atmosphere in one place at one particular time. Climate is the usual weather in a particular place over a long time. For example, the weather may change each day in Fresno, California from rainy to windy or sunny. But the general climate does not change. In a usual year, Fresno has a hot, dry summer and a mild, rainy winter. Brownsville, Texas may have a hot, dry Monday in July and a hot, rainy Tuesday in July, but the climate is the same year after year. In a usual year, Brownsville has a hot, rainy summer and a hot, dry winter.

Climate is the usual, or average, weather in a particular place over a long time.

Why are climates different in different parts of the world? The usual climate of a particular area is caused by five different things. One climate-maker is **latitude**. How close is the area to the equator? How close is it to the poles? A second climate-maker is **elevation**. How high above the level of the sea is the area? Is the area 5,000 feet up on a mountain? Or is the area on a low, flat desert? Distance from water is the third cause of climate. Is the area on the coast of a great ocean? Is it next to a large lake? The fourth thing that determines an area's climate is its position on a continent. Is it in the central part of a large continent? Is it on the east or west edge of a large continent? The fifth climate-maker is the pattern of the winds in the area. In which direction do the winds usually blow? How often do the winds blow? How strongly?

All of these things—latitude, elevation, distance from water, position on a continent, and wind patterns—help determine what the climate will be for the area where you live.

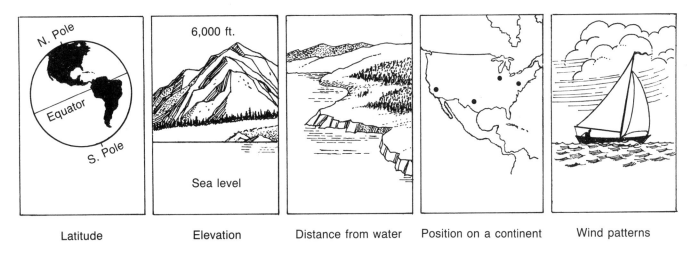

| Latitude | Elevation | Distance from water | Position on a continent | Wind patterns |

What determines the climate of a particular area?

SELF-EVALUATION 1

VOCABULARY TICKETS

Read the vocabulary tickets with your teacher and the whole class. Are there still some words you do not understand? Write these words in a notebook. With a partner, write some example sentences using these new words. Talk about the meaning of these words with your classmates.

VOCABULARY CHECK

Here are some important words from this reading. Do you understand all of these words? Circle the words you do not understand. Then find the words in the reading. Talk about the meaning of these words with your classmates. If you know all the words, continue to the Question Review.

atmosphere   latitude
climate   moisture
elevation   weather

PRE-READING 2

FOCUS QUESTION

Skim the reading on pages 8, 9, and 10 to find the answer to the question below. Underline the answer in your book. Write the answer below.

■ *What are the steps that make up the water cycle?* _____

_____

DETAIL QUESTIONS

LEARNING STRATEGY
☆ **Reading selectively**

Read "The Water Cycle" on pages 8, 9, and 10. Find the details. Underline the answers in your book. Write the answers below. As you read, write down on your vocabulary tickets any words you do not understand or cannot pronounce.

1. What is water vapor? _____

_____

2. What happens to raindrops that fall into very dry weather?

_____

_____

3. What happens to ice crystals that fall from a cloud into very

warm air? _____

_____

READING 2 ★

The Water Cycle

Where do clouds and rain come from? How are they made? To learn how clouds and rain are made, you should first understand four rules of nature.

1. Warm air rises and cool air falls. Warm air is lighter than cold air.

2. Heat causes water to turn into a gas called **water vapor**. This changing of water into a gas is called **evaporation**.

3. When warm water vapor rises and meets cold air, the water vapor settles on tiny **particles** of dust in the air and changes back into water drops. This changing of water vapor back into water drops is called **condensation**.

4. When condensation becomes heavy, the water falls back to earth. This falling of water back to earth is called **precipitation**.

The group observations demonstrated these rules of nature. Why did the water disappear from the dish you left in the sun? Why was more water left in the dish that was put in the shade? What happened to the moist dirt that was left in the sun for two days? Were these examples of condensation or evaporation?

You filled a glass with ice and water and left it for 10 minutes. What happened to the glass? Water drops appeared on the outside of the glass. This is an example of condensation. Ice cools the air around the glass. The water vapor in the warm air of a room touches the cold glass and changes back into water. It condenses on the cold glass.

Why, then, does ice cream stay frozen in an open-topped freezer? Why does the cold air not escape out into the room and let the ice cream become warm? Does cold air rise or fall? Cold air falls. Warm air rises and escapes into the room. The cold air stays in the freezer.

When these four rules of nature are put together they are called the water cycle.

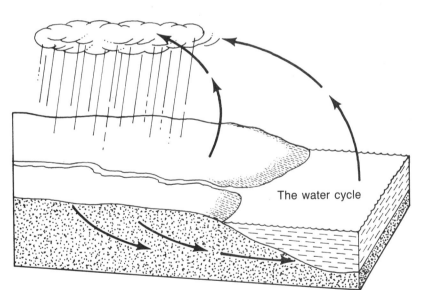

The water cycle

The earth is warmed by rays from the sun. The heat from the earth evaporates moisture into the air making water vapor. This warm, moist air rises high into the sky where it mixes with very cold air. The warm air cools, and the water vapor settles on dust particles in the air and condenses—it changes to tiny drops of water. A cloud is made of millions of tiny water drops. When the cloud gets too heavy with raindrops, the rain falls and there is precipitation.

Not all precipitation is rain. Sometimes water vapor high above the earth is very cold. It forms a cloud made of pieces of ice called **ice crystals**. When the ice crystals come together and become heavy they fall to earth. If the air below the ice crystal cloud is warm, the ice will melt and fall as rain. But, if the air below the ice crystal cloud is very cold all the way down, the precipitation will be snow. Sometimes the precipitation that falls from a cloud never even reaches the earth! If the air is very dry below a cloud, the raindrops may evaporate and rise up again before hitting the ground.

You may want to try to make your own cloud at home. Put a pot of water on the stove and bring it to a boil. Hot, moist air will form a cloud of water vapor above the pot. The water vapor cloud will rise up and meet colder air in the room. You may see drops of condensation form on the ceiling. If you let the water boil for a long time, this condensation will become heavy and form "raindops" that fall from the ceiling.

The three steps: evaporation, condensation, and precipitation make up the water cycle in nature.

SELF-EVALUATION 2

VOCABULARY TICKETS

Read the vocabulary tickets with your teacher and the whole class. Are there still some words you do not understand? Write these words in a notebook. With a partner, write some example sentences using these new words. Talk about the meaning of these words with your classmates.

VOCABULARY CHECK

Here are some important words from this reading. Do you understand all of these words? Circle the words you do not understand. Then find the words in the reading. Talk about the meaning of these words with your classmates. If you know all the words, continue to the Question Review.

condensation	particles
evaporation	precipitation
ice crystals	water vapor

QUESTION REVIEW

Go back to the questions on page 8. Look at your answers. Work with a partner. Look at your partner's answers too. Are they the same as your answers? Help each other write the correct answers.

PRE-READING 3

FOCUS QUESTION

Skim the reading on pages 11, 12, and 13 to find the answer to the question below. Underline the answer in your book. Write the answer below.

■ *What are the names of three main kinds of clouds?* _____

_____

DETAIL QUESTIONS

Read "Clouds" on pages 11, 12, and 13. Find the details. Underline the answers in your book. Write the answers below. As you read, write down on your vocabulary tickets any words you do not understand or cannot pronounce.

LEARNING STRATEGY
☆ **Reading selectively**

1. What is the name for a person who studies and reports the weather?

   _____

   _____

2. What does a cumulus cloud look like? _____

   _____

3. Where do you often see cumulus clouds? _____

   _____

4. Describe a stratus cloud. _____

   _____

5. Where in the sky are you most likely to find a cirrus cloud?

   _____

   _____

6. What is a cirrus cloud made of? _____

   _____

READING 3 ★

Clouds

Clouds come in many different sizes and shapes. Some clouds look solid, gray, and flat. Others look like soft, white cotton. Still others are like long, thin strings. Clouds form at all different heights above the earth. A cloud's height above the surface of the sea is called its **altitude**. Some are miles high, others are close to the ground. Each type of cloud has a special name. They are named by the way they look and by their altitude or position in the sky. A **meteorologist** is a person who studies the weather and reports it to us. Clouds help meteorologists **predict**, or know about, future weather.

There are three conditions that cause air to rise and clouds to form in the sky.

1. If the surface of the earth is warm, the air becomes warm and rises. As it rises, it cools and forms a cloud.

2. Sometimes cold air will blow in under warmer air and push the warm air up. The air cools as it rises and forms a cloud.

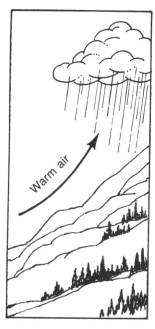

3. Sometimes warm air moves sideways over land or water and then bumps into a mountain. It is forced to move up instead of sideways. It cools as it rises and forms a cloud.

The three main kinds of clouds are **cumulus**, **stratus**, and **cirrus**. Cumulus clouds look like thick, fluffy cotton on top. They are flat and gray on the bottom. They are usually separate from other clouds. Cumulus clouds are usually low-altitude clouds that often appear over mountain tops. But they are also seen in other places over land and water. Usually you see cumulus clouds on a warm, sunny day. They are called "fair-weather" clouds.

Stratus clouds are dark gray and look stretched out. Stratus clouds cover a large area of the sky. They are flat on the bottom and on top. They may look like a long, smooth sheet at a low altitude in the sky. Clouds of this kind are common near the coasts of the United States, especially in California and Oregon. A stratus cloud is a layer of tiny water drops. Stratus clouds might bring light rain called **drizzle**, but they almost never bring rain.

Cirrus clouds are very high up in the sky. The temperature there is always below freezing. Cirrus clouds look like feathers or thin curls of hair that have been brushed. They are made of ice crystals. These icy clouds often form at night.

Cumulus

Stratus

Cirrus

Sometimes it is possible to see all three kinds of these clouds in the sky at one time. Find the cumulus, stratus, and cirrus clouds in the picture.

SELF-EVALUATION 3

VOCABULARY TICKETS

Read the vocabulary tickets with your teacher and the whole class. Are there still some words you do not understand? Write these words in a notebook. With a partner, write some example sentences using these new words. Talk about the meaning of these words with your classmates.

VOCABULARY CHECK

Here are some important words from this reading. Do you understand all of these words? Circle the words you do not understand. Then find the words in the reading. Talk about the meaning of these words with your classmates. If you know all the words, continue to the Question Review.

altitude	drizzle	predict
cirrus	meteorologist	stratus
cumulus		

QUESTION REVIEW

Go back to the questions on pages 10 and 11. Look at your answers. Work with a partner. Look at your partner's answers too. Are they the same as your answers? Help each other write the correct answers.

PRE-READING 4

FOCUS QUESTION

Skim the reading on pages 15 and 16 to find the answer to the question below. Underline the answer in your book. Write the answer below.

■ *What are the five main kinds of climates?* _____

_____

DETAIL QUESTIONS

LEARNING STRATEGY
☆ **Reading selectively**

Read "World Climates" on pages 15 and 16. Find the details. Underline the answers in your book. As you read, write down on your vocabulary tickets any words you do not understand or cannot pronounce.

1. Between which latitudes are most tropical climates? _____

_____

2. What are two kinds of tropical climates? _____

_____

3. Where are the polar climates located? _____

_____

4. What kind of climate is found on the West Coast of the United

States? _____

_____

5. In which latitudes do we find a continental climate? _____

_____

6. Why are there very few continental climate areas in the Southern

Hemisphere? _____

_____

World Climates

In the northern part of Canada, the air is always cold. In northwestern Africa, the air is always very hot and dry. In the central coast region of California, the air is almost always mild. Wouldn't it be wonderful if all parts of the world had a sunny, warm, California coast climate? No, not really. Different kinds of climates are very important to the earth. Air from cold regions, for example, mixes with air from warm places to make the rain that is needed to grow food for countries in the middle latitudes.

The world is divided into several climate zones, or regions. They are divided according to their usual temperature and the amount of rainfall they have. The five main types of climate are a **tropical climate**, a **mild climate**, a **dry climate**, a **polar climate**, and a **continental climate**.

TROPICAL CLIMATE
Maui, Hawaii

MILD CLIMATE
San Francisco,
California

DRY CLIMATE
Salt Lake City, Utah

POLAR CLIMATE
Barrow, Alaska

CONTINENTAL
CLIMATE
Chicago, Illinois

Look at a map of the world. Find the **equator**. Find the **Tropic of Cancer** in the **Northern Hemisphere** at 23½° latitude. Find the **Tropic of Capricorn** in the **Southern Hemisphere**. The area between 23½° north latitude and 23½° south latitude is called the tropics or the low latitudes. The climate of this area is called a tropical climate. Some regions with tropical climates are hot and rainy all year round. Other tropical climate regions are hot all year round but have rain only in the summer months. Examples of places with tropical climates are Ecuador, the Philippines, northern Australia, and Senegal, Africa.

Look at the map again. Find the **Arctic Circle** and the **Antarctic Circle** at 67° north latitude and 67° south latitude. The areas from these circles toward the poles have short, cool summers and very long, cold winters. They have a polar climate. Some regions with a polar climate have just enough warmth in the summer to grow a few small plants. Other polar climate areas are covered with ice that is several thousand feet deep year round. No plants can grow in these areas. Iceland, Siberia, Antarctica, and Greenland have polar climates.

In the middle latitudes, between 30° and 60° north and south, are mild climates of three different kinds. The mild climate areas next to the ocean on the west coasts of a continent have cool summers and mild winters with only a little rain throughout the year. This mild climate is found on the west coasts of France and California. Other mild climate regions have a warm, rainy winter and a hot, dry summer. Southern Italy and Spain have this kind of mild climate. The third kind of mild climate is found in southeastern regions of large continents, such as in the states of Louisiana and Florida in the United States. This mild climate has warm winters, very hot and humid, or wet, summers, and rainfall all year. Southeastern China and southeastern Africa also have this kind of mild climate.

Dry climate regions have very little rainfall. Many large plants or trees cannot grow in these regions. The central flat land of the United States has a dry climate. Only short grasses can grow there. Dry climates of the desert areas, such as in northern Mexico and northern Africa, sometimes have no rainfall for many years. Desert areas may be cold or hot depending on their elevation and their latitude.

Finally, there is the continental climate that is found in the central and eastern parts of large continents in the middle latitudes, between 40° and the Arctic Circle. There are two kinds of continental climate areas: regions with a short, cool summer and a long, cold winter, such as in southern Alaska, and regions with a warm summer and a cold winter, such as in the states of New York, Illinois, and North Dakota. Notice that continental climates are found mostly in the Northern Hemisphere. Why? Look at a map of the world. As you can see, there is very little land in the Southern Hemisphere south of 40° latitude!

What kind of climate does the area you live in have?

SELF-EVALUATION 4

VOCABULARY TICKETS   Read the vocabulary tickets with your teacher and the whole class. Are there still some words you do not understand? Write these words in a notebook. With a partner, write some example sentences using these new words. Talk about the meaning of these words with your classmates.

VOCABULARY CHECK

Here are some important words from this reading. Do you understand all of these words? Circle the words you do not understand. Then find the words in the reading. Talk about the meaning of these words with your classmates. If you know all the words, continue to the Question Review.

Antarctic Circle	Northern Hemisphere
Arctic Circle	polar climate
continental climate	Southern Hemisphere
dry climate	Tropic of Cancer
equator	Tropic of Capricorn
mild climate	tropical climate

QUESTION REVIEW

Go back to the questions on page 14. Look at your answers. Work with a partner. Look at your partner's answers too. Are they the same as your answers? Help each other write the correct answers.

CHAPTER REVIEW

Now that you have completed your reading about climate and weather, go back to pages 2, 3, and 4. Look at your first ideas about climate and weather. Have your ideas changed? What have you learned? Talk about your ideas with the teacher and the whole class.

EXTENSION ACTIVITIES

A. WEATHER EXPERIMENTS

LEARNING STRATEGIES
☆ **Inferencing**
☆ **Working cooperatively**

Materials

a large coffee can	2 small plastic flower pots
a large thermometer	a pie tin
a small kitchen scale	2 boxes of salt
a tall, thin glass	a piece of cardboard
a bag of ice cubes	2 cups of dirt
a sponge	a measuring cup

1. Making frost. Fill the coffee can with alternate layers of ice cubes and salt. The ice and salt must be packed very tightly and closely in the can. You will see condensation, or some water on the outside of the can. The water will freeze. After a short time, you will see that the can is covered by very thin, white, frost crystals.

2. Measuring the temperature of the soil. Take a large thermometer outside. Find a place where the sun has been shining on the dirt for at least two hours. Carefully push the end of the thermometer into the dirt. Leave it in the dirt for three minutes. Write down the temperature of the dirt. Then find a place where the dirt has been in the shade for at least two hours and measure the temperature. Write down the temperature of the shaded dirt. Compare the two temperatures. Explain why the dirt in the sun has a different temperature from the dirt in the shade.

3. Area and evaporation. Measure out exactly one cup of water and pour it into a tall, thin glass. Then pour out another cup of water into a pie tin. Place the two containers side by side where they will get the same amount of sun and air. After 24 hours, carefully pour the water from the glass back into the measuring cup. How much water is left? Then pour the water from the pie tin back into the measuring cup. How much water is left? Compare how much water is left in each container. Explain what happened.

4. Moving air and evaporation. With a wet sponge, make a spot on the blackboard about one foot square. On the other end of the blackboard (or on a different board) make another wet spot the same size as the first one. Stand in front of one of the wet spots and fan it with a piece of cardboard. Do not fan the other spot. After a few minutes compare the two spots. What is the difference? Explain what happened.

5. Water in the soil. Put an equal amount of dirt in each of the small plastic pots. Wet the soil in both pots with an equal amount of water. Weigh the pots on the kitchen scale. Both pots must weigh the same. Write down the weight of each pot. Put one pot in a sunny window and the other pot away from the sun. After 24 hours, weigh the pots again. Compare the weights. How have they changed? Explain what happened.

6. Weather chart. Keep a weather chart in your classroom for two weeks. At the same time each day record the outdoor temperature. Record the types of clouds you see in the sky and their location. Record whether there is wind and from which direction it is coming. Record if there is any kind of precipitation such as rain, drizzle, or snow.

    In groups of four, design a chart where you can write all this information. It should be a chart that is organized and easy to read and understand. Each group's chart may be different as long as the information is recorded.

B. VOCABULARY REVIEW   Work in groups. With your partners fill in the vocabulary words from Chapter 1.

1. Another name for rain is _____.

2. When water rises into the air and turns into a gas, the gas is called _____.

3. The imaginary line around the earth at its widest part is the _____.

4. The important difference between weather and climate is _____.

5. A gray cloud that is flat on the top and bottom is

_____ .

6. Two words that describe the distance above the level of the sea are

_____ and _____ .

7. A person who studies, predicts, and reports the weather is a

_____ .

8. A _____ cloud is a fair-weather cloud.

9. _____ clouds are very high-altitude

clouds and are made of ice crystals.

GLOSSARY

altitude Height above the level of the surface of the sea.

Antarctic Circle The area around the South Pole at 67° south latitude.

Arctic Circle The area around the North Pole at 67° north latitude.

atmosphere Air.

cirrus A thin, high-altitude cloud made of ice crystals that looks like brushed, white curls of hair.

climate The condition of the atmosphere in one place over a long period of time.

condensation The changing of water vapor (a gas) back into drops of water.

continental climate The usual climate of the central and eastern part of a large continent; regions with this climate may have a short, cool summer and a long, cold winter, or they may have a hot summer and a cold winter.

cumulus A fair-weather cloud that looks like thick, white cotton on top and is flat and gray on the bottom.

drizzle A fine, light rain.

dry climate A climate with very little or no rainfall; a region with a dry climate can be hot or cold depending on its latitude and elevation.

elevation The height above the level of the sea; altitude.

equator An imaginary line around the earth at its widest part; 0° latitude.

evaporation The changing of water to a gas that rises in the air.

ice crystals Frozen pieces of ice that are found in very high-altitude clouds.

latitudes Imaginary lines drawn around the earth that divide it into sections, or degrees, and are measures of the distance north or south of the equator.

meteorologist A person who studies, predicts, and reports the weather.

mild climate The usual climate of the middle latitudes, 30° to 60° north or south. Regions with mild climates can have: cool summers, mild winters and a little rainfall all year round; a warm, rainy winter and a hot, dry summer; or warm winters, hot, wet summers and rainfall all year round.

moisture Wetness, dampness, having water.

North Pole 90° north latitude; the exact top of the planet.

Northern Hemisphere The northern, or top half, of the planet.

particles Very tiny parts; parts that may be too small to see without a microscope.

polar circles 67° latitude, north and south.

polar climate The usual climate from 67° latitude north and south to the poles; a climate with short, cool summers and long, cold winters.

precipitation Drizzle, rain, sleet, or snow that falls to earth.

predict Tell what will happen in the future.

South Pole 90° south latitude; the exact bottom of the planet.

Southern Hemisphere The southern, or bottom half, of the planet.

stratus A dark-gray cloud that is flat on the top and bottom; it is usually a low-altitude cloud.

Tropic of Cancer 23½° north latitude.

Tropic of Capricorn 23½° south latitude.

tropical climate Climate of the low latitudes, between the Tropic of Cancer and the Tropic of Capricorn; regions with this climate are hot and rainy all year round, or they are hot all year with rain only in the summer months.

water vapor A gas made up of tiny drops of water.

weather The condition of the air in one place at one particular time.

2 TOPOGRAPHY

THE UNITED STATES LANDSCAPE

INTRODUCTION

Topography is the study of the surface of the earth. The surface of the earth is divided into **natural regions**. Each natural region has its own **features**, such as mountains, valleys, lakes, and rivers. The features of a region make up its **landscape**. There are many different kinds of landscapes on the earth. There are hot, dry desert landscapes. There are cool, high mountain landscapes. There are wide, green **valley** landscapes. In this chapter you will learn about the natural regions of the United States. You will read and talk about the landscapes of a few of these regions. You will find out names and locations of some of the mountains, **volcanoes**, rivers, and **lakes** of the United States, and learn about what causes the different features of a landscape.

WHAT DO YOU ALREADY KNOW ABOUT THE UNITED STATES LANDSCAPE?

Read these sentences. Draw a circle around the words you do not understand. Underline the words you cannot pronounce.

> The United States is a large country.
>
> In the United States there are many mountain ranges.
>
> Some regions in the United States are deserts.
>
> There are five very large lakes in the northern part of the United States.
>
> The United States is bordered on the west by the Pacific Ocean and on the east by the Atlantic Ocean.

Sit down with a partner. Look at your book and your partner's book. Help each other understand the words that are circled. Help each other pronounce the words that are underlined.

THINK ABOUT THESE IDEAS

Work in groups of three or four. Work together to do the activity. If you are not sure about the answers, guess!

☐ Look at the pictures. Read the words below. Choose the correct word for each picture.

Lake	Mountain	Desert
Volcano	Valley	Mountain range

When your group finishes talking about these ideas, share your ideas with the whole class. Are your ideas different? Are they similar? After you read this chapter look at these ideas again. Do not worry if your answers are right or wrong.

GROUP OBSERVATIONS

LEARNING STRATEGIES
☆ **Working cooperatively**
☆ **Grouping**
☆ **Self-evaluation**

There are as many as 70,000 different kinds of **soil** in the United States. Soil is made of broken down rock. It is also made of organic material. Organic material is material that was once alive, such as insects, plants, and animals. When dead trees and leaves and plants fall to the ground, they are mixed with the broken down rock and different kinds of soil are formed. Do the following observation exercise to compare (see how soils are similar) and contrast (see how soils are different).

Materials

> 1 cupful of two different kinds of soil for each student
> glass jars for the soil
> paper plates
> a magnifying glass
> a teaspoon
> a ruler

When you come to class tomorrow, bring one cupful of two different kinds of soil and a teaspoon. Put the two kinds of soil in two clear glass jars. Look for your soil samples in two different locations, such as a field, a garden, a park, or next to a river. Write down where you found the soil.

1. Sit down in groups of three. With your group, put the six soil samples on paper plates, mark each plate with a different number. Study the soil samples under a magnifying glass.

   Check the texture of the soils. How do they feel? Put a half teaspoon of each kind of soil on a piece of white paper. Rub the soil between your fingers. Do the different soils feel sandy, rocky, or smooth? Are they made of sharp pieces or rounded pieces? Are the pieces large or fine? Also look for parts of plants or insects in the soils. You may find pieces of leaves or roots. Check the color of each sample.

   Write some sentences in your notebook describing your observation of the color and texture of the six soils.

2. Next, you will test the six soils to see what each soil is made of. Label each jar with the soil numbers and the locations where they were found. Add enough water to fill the jar. Stir the soil and water well. Let the soil stand in the jar until the water above the soil is almost clear. Compare the jars of soil. You should see sand and small rocks on the bottom. The middle layer will be silt or mud. Very small grains of clay may be on top. You may see organic material floating on the top of the water.

Record the results of your observation in the following way:

1. Cut two pieces of paper in strips about 3 inches by 8 inches.
2. Give each strip the same numbers as the soil samples.
3. Measure the thickness of each layer of soil in each jar with a ruler.
4. Draw these measurements on one of the strips of paper. Look at the example given here.
5. Color in the layers and label them "sand," "silt," "clay," and "organic material." Do the same with each sample.

Share your answers with the whole class. After you finish reading this chapter, come back to these questions and observations and read them again. Are your answers the same?

PRE-READING 1

FOCUS QUESTION

Skim the reading on pages 25, 26, and 27 to find the answer to the question below. Underline the answer in your book. Write the answer below.

■ *What are the three major kinds of landscapes in the United*

States? _____

_____

DETAIL QUESTIONS

Read "Plains, Plateaus, and Mountains" on pages 25, 26, and 27. Find the details. Underline the answers in your book. As you read, write down on your vocabulary tickets any words you do not understand or cannot pronounce.

LEARNING STRATEGY
☆ Reading selectively

1. How is a plateau different from a plain? _____

_____

2. What features make up a mountain landscape? _____

_____

3. What river formed the Grand Canyon? _____

_____

Plains, Plateaus, and Mountains

In the United States, and in other parts of the world, the surface of the land varies, or changes, from place to place. If you could see the United States from a spaceship, you would see how the **features** of a **landscape** change from one part of the country to another. The map shows 13 different **natural regions** of the United States. Each region is very different from the other. It is easy to see on a map where one region ends and the next one begins. In some areas, gentle hills and **valleys** and slow moving rivers make up the landscape. In the western part of the United States, there is a long mountain **range**, or line of high mountains, called Sierra Nevada. The southern part of Texas is a flat, **coastal plain**. In which region do you live? Have you ever visited a different region of the United States?

There are three major kinds of landscapes in the United States: **plains, plateaus**, and **mountain areas**. Find these landscapes on the map.

Plains are large, level areas. Flat plains make up about one-half of the land area of the United States.

Plateaus make up about one-fourth of the land area of the United States. A plateau is also a large, flat area but it is higher up than the land that surrounds it. The height, or **elevation**, of a plateau is greater than that of a plain. Elevation is measured as the distance above the level of the ocean, or **sea level**.

Mountain areas make up about one-fourth of the land area of the United States. This landscape has high mountain peaks separated by deep valleys and shallow valleys. A shallow valley is called a **basin**.

In the western part of the United States there are three natural regions. They are the Great Plains, the Rocky Mountains, and the Colorado Plateau. Find these three regions on the map to the right.

The Great Plains region is a large, flat area in the central United States. This giant region runs from Canada in the north to parts of Texas in the South. It covers about 450,000 square miles (1,165,000 square kilometers). There is little variation or change across the landscape of the Great Plains. You can stand and look across 30 miles or more of land that is all the same elevation. This region has very little rain.

The Rocky Mountains, often called the Rockies, are made up of several mountain ranges. These mountain ranges run through Canada in the north to New Mexico in the south. Find the Rockies on the map. This region has a landscape that has many different features. There are deep valleys and basins. There are high mountain peaks that rise to an elevation of more than 14,000 feet (4,300 meters) above sea level.

This mountain region is divided into three parts: the Northern, Middle, and Southern Rockies. These separate ranges of mountains are not alike. They have different rock arrangements, different kinds of rocks, and different elevations. How many separate mountain ranges can you find in the illustration of the Rockies?

The Colorado Plateau is hot, flat, and dry. It is in the southwestern part of the United States. It covers an area of about 58,000 square miles (150,000 square kilometers). It has an average elevation of over 5000 feet (1,500 meters) above sea level. The plateau has been deeply cut over millions of years by very fast moving streams and rivers such as the Colorado River. The most famous of these deep cuts is a **canyon** called the Grand Canyon. There are many unusual features and rock formations in the region of the Colorado Plateau.

The United States is a very large country and is made up of many different and interesting landscapes.

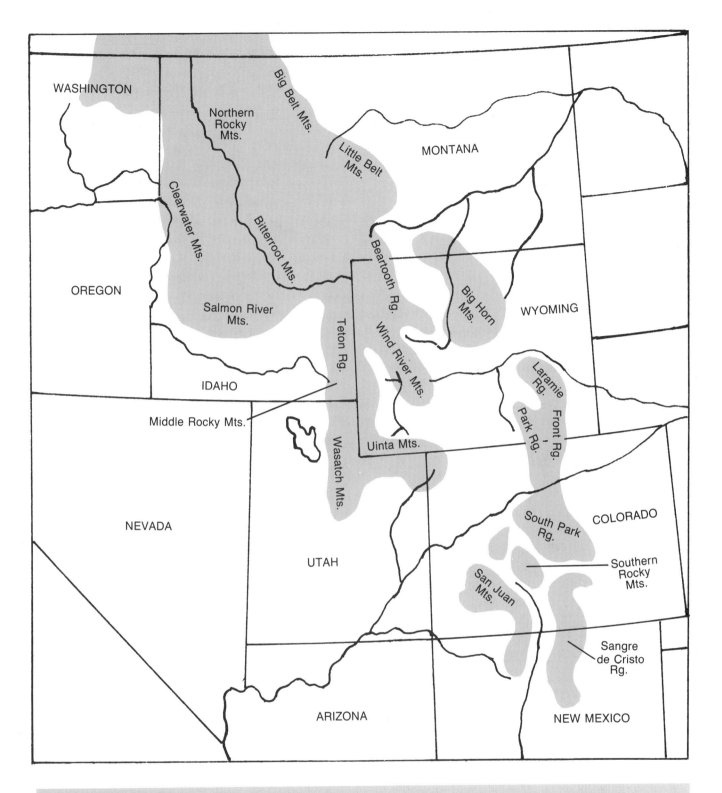

SELF-EVALUATION 1

VOCABULARY TICKETS   Read the vocabulary tickets with your teacher and the whole class. Are there still some words you do not understand? Write these words in a notebook. With a partner, write some example sentences using these new words. Talk about the meaning of these words with your classmates.

VOCABULARY CHECK

Here are some important words from this reading. Do you understand all of these words? Circle the words you do not understand. Then find the words in the reading. Talk about the meaning of these words with your classmates. If you know all the words, continue to the Question Review.

basin	natural regions
canyon	plains
coastal plain	plateaus
elevation	range
features	sea level
landscape	valleys
mountain areas	

QUESTION REVIEW

Go back to the questions on page 24. Look at your answers. Work with a partner. Look at your partner's answers too. Are they the same as your answers? Help each other write the correct answers.

PRE-READING 2

FOCUS QUESTION

Skim the reading on pages 29, 30, and 31 to find the answer to the question below. Underline the answer in your book. Write the answer below.

■ *What is a drainage basin?* _____

_____

DETAIL QUESTIONS

Read "Water on the Land" on pages 29, 30, and 31. Find the details. Underline the answers in your book. Write the answers below. As you read, write down on your vocabulary tickets any words you do not understand or cannot pronounce.

> **LEARNING STRATEGY**
>
> ☆ **Reading selectively**

1. How is still water different from running water? _____

_____

2. What is a very small body of still water called? _____

_____

3. What is the difference between a river and a creek? _____

_____

4. Lakes may be deep or shallow. What is the deepest lake shown in the table on page 31? Where is this lake? What is one unusual

thing about this lake? _____

_____

Water on the Land

Running water and **still water** are a part of almost every landscape. Running water is water that moves. After raindrops hit the ground, they run together. They form small **creeks** and larger **streams** that begin to move downhill. The streams run into even larger rivers.

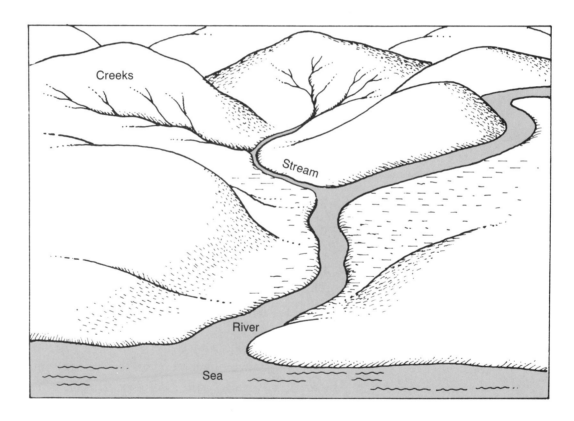

An area of small creeks and streams where rain water collects is called a **drainage basin**. Smaller drainage basins are usually a part of a larger basin. Each large drainage basin system has a major river that carries water away to the ocean or a large **lake**. These rivers move water through a region. The map on the next page shows the major rivers in the United States. Rivers on the west side of the Rocky Mountains move westward to the Pacific Ocean. East of the Rockies, the rivers move to the Gulf of Mexico or the Atlantic Ocean.

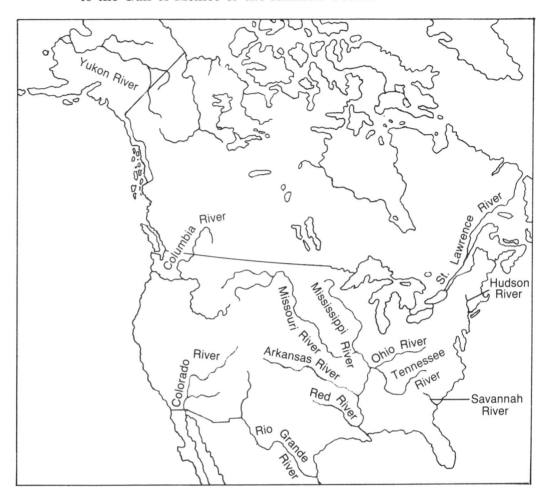

Still water is water that stays in one place on the land. It is not running or moving water. Small **ponds** and larger lakes are examples of still water. The table on the next page lists the 12 largest freshwater lakes in the world. Eight of these lakes are in North America.

The shallow lakes were formed in areas where running water or ice on the land carried away some of the rock millions of years ago. These low areas then filled up with water to form the great shallow lakes, such as Lake Erie and Lake Winnepeg in North America.

Deep lakes were formed by water running into natural low spots on the earth's surface. Lake Baikal in Russia is a very interesting deep-water lake. It is nearly 5,317 feet deep (1,595 meters) and has over 1,500 kinds of plant and animal life. Most of these plants and animals are not found anywhere else on earth! Lake Baikal is nearly 1,000 miles (1,600 kilometers) away from the ocean, but among the animals that live there are seals. Seals, of course, are usually found only in the ocean!

Running water and still water are an important feature of most natural regions. Rivers and lakes provide water for industry, farming, drinking, and recreation.

The 12 largest freshwater lakes in the world

Name	Location	Area (square kilometers)	Maximum depth (meters)
Superior	N. America	82,103	400
Victoria	Africa	69,485	80
Huron	N. America	59,829	225
Michigan	N. America	57,757	277
Tanganyika	Africa	32,893	1,395
Great Bear	N. America	31,328	407
Baikal	Asia	30,510	1,595
Nyasa	Africa	29,604	668
Great Slave	N. America	28,570	605
Erie	N. America	25,667	63
Winnipeg	N. America	24,390	18
Ontario	N. America	19,555	241

SELF-EVALUATION 2

VOCABULARY TICKETS

Read the vocabulary tickets with your teacher and the whole class. Are there still some words you do not understand? Write these words in a notebook. With a partner, write some example sentences using these new words. Talk about the meaning of these words with your classmates.

VOCABULARY CHECK

Here are some important words from this reading. Do you understand all of these words? Circle the words you do not understand. Then find the words in the reading. Talk about the meaning of these words with your classmates. If you know all the words, continue to the Question Review.

creeks   running water

drainage basin   still water

lake   streams

ponds

QUESTION REVIEW

Go back to the questions on pages 28 and 29. Look at your answers. Work with a partner. Look at your partner's answers too. Are they the same as your answers? Help each other write the correct answers.

PRE-READING 3

FOCUS QUESTION

Skim the reading on pages 32, 33, 34, and 35 to find the answer to the question below. Underline the answer in your book. Write the answer below.

■ *What shapes the landscape of a region?* _____

_____

DETAIL QUESTIONS

| **LEARNING STRATEGY** |
| ☆ Reading selectively |

Read "What Causes the Different Kinds of Landscapes?" on pages 32, 33, 34, and 35. Find the details. Underline the answers in your book. Write the answers below. As you read, write down on your vocabulary tickets any words you do not understand or cannot pronounce.

1. What causes erosion? _____

_____

2. What is uplift? _____

_____

3. What geologic process causes volcanoes to form? _____

_____

4. What kind of mountains are the Cascade Range? Where are they

located? _____

_____

READING 3 ★

What Causes the Different Kinds of Landscapes?

The earth's surface has many different faces. It may be level and low or level and high. It may be a mixture of tall peaks and deep canyons and valleys. It may be covered with trees and grasses or it may have no plant life at all.

Geologic processes form the landscape of a region. Geologic processes are natural changes or movements that happen inside or on the earth over millions of years. Three important kinds of geologic processes are **erosion**, **uplift**, and **volcanism**.

Erosion takes place when wind or running water removes the **topsoil** on the surface of the earth. It is the wearing away, or carrying away, of the soil. Natural erosion can cause some interesting and beautiful land features. But erosion can also destroy the land. For example, erosion can carry away the rich topsoil that is needed for farmland. Erosion may happen over many years as a natural geologic process. It may also happen very quickly if a region is not taken care of by the people who live there.

Beautiful landforms in Bryce Canyon in Utah

A natural geologic process that happened too quickly

Uplift is the rising of parts of the earth's surface caused by **pressures**. A pressure is a pushing and squeezing of rock deep in the earth. These

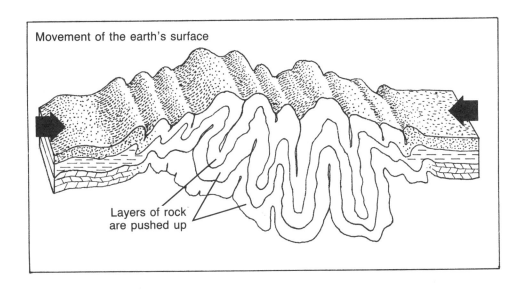

Movement of the earth's surface

Layers of rock are pushed up

pressures cause the rock to fold, crack, and move upward. This slow but constant movement of rock forms many different kinds of mountains.

Volcanism is the geologic process that forms **volcanoes**. Inside the earth there is hot, liquid rock called **magma**. Magma rises up and **erupts**, or comes out, onto the surface of the earth through a hole, or vent. Volcanism is the power or action of this magma as it is thrown out and builds volcanic mountains. When the magma is out on the surface of the earth, it is called **lava**.

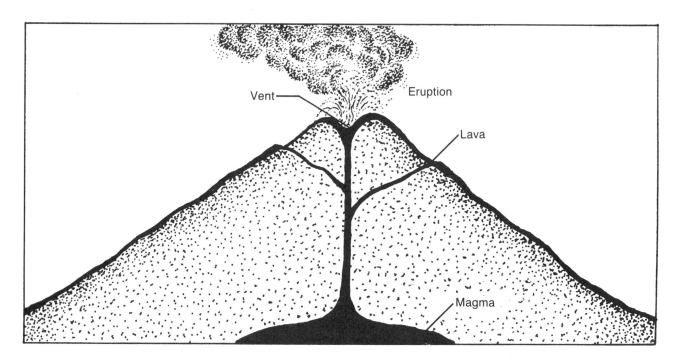

Cross section of a volcano

There are many volcanoes in the Cascade Mountain range in the states of Washington, Oregon, and California. Fifteen of the peaks in the Cascades are volcanoes, but most of them have been inactive, or quiet, in recent years.

However, in 1980 the land around Mt. St. Helens began to shake. There were many small **earthquakes**. In March of 1980, some steam and powdery rock materials called ash came out of the top of the mountain. Then, on May 18 there were two strong earthquakes and Mt. St. Helens exploded! It was the largest eruption, or volcanic explosion, in all of U. S. history. Millions of tons of rock and ash flew as high as twelve miles into the air. This ash and dust fell back to earth as far as 500 miles away.

Many houses, cars, and bridges were destroyed. More than 20 people were killed and over 100 were reported missing. Today Mt. St. Helens is still active. It may be active for many more years.

Eruption of Mt. St. Helens

Three important geologic processes to remember are erosion, uplift, and volcanism. These geologic processes help to shape the landscape.

SELF-EVALUATION 3

VOCABULARY TICKETS

Read the vocabulary tickets with your teacher and the whole class. Are there still some words you do not understand? Write these words in a notebook. With a partner, write some example sentences using these new words. Talk about the meaning of these words with your classmates.

VOCABULARY CHECK

Here are some important words from this reading. Do you understand all of these words? Circle the words you do not understand. Then find the words in the reading. Talk about the meaning of these words with your classmates. If you know all the words, continue to the Question Review.

earthquakes   pressures

erosion   topsoil

erupts   uplift

geologic processes   volcanism

lava   volcanoes

magma

QUESTION REVIEW

Go back to the questions on pages 31 and 32. Look at your answers. Work with a partner. Look at your partner's answers too. Are they the same as your answers? Help each other write the correct answers.

FOCUS QUESTION

Skim the reading on pages 36, 37, 38, and 39 to find the answer to the question below. Underline the answer in your book. Write the answer below.

■ *What is rock structure?* _____

_____

DETAIL QUESTIONS

LEARNING STRATEGY
☆ **Reading selectively**

Read "Rock Structure and Kinds of Rock" on pages 36, 37, 38, and 39. Find the details. Underline the answers in your book. As you read, write down on your vocabulary tickets any words you do not understand or cannot pronounce. Write the answers below.

1. Name three kinds of rock. _____

_____

2. How is igneous rock formed? _____

_____

3. What is sedimentary rock formed from? _____

_____

4. What does the word *metamorphic* mean? _____

_____

READING 4 ★

Rock Structure and Kinds of Rock

Water on the land, erosion, uplift, and volcanism all shape the landscape. **Rock structure** is the arrangement of rock below the surface of the earth. It is another thing that shapes a landscape. In a mountain area, the rock below the surface of the earth may be moved **vertically**, or pushed upward. It may be lifted high above sea level by the natural movement of the earth over many years. The rock of a coastal plain may be pushed **horizontally**, or sideways. The rock structure causes many different features and elevations in landscape.

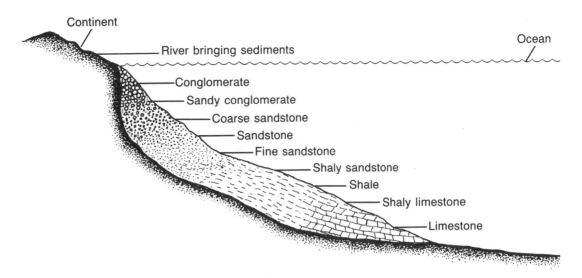

Horizontal layers of sedimentary rock

The kind of rock found in a region helps shape that region, too. There are three kinds of rock: **igneous rock**, **sedimentary rock**, and **metamorphic rock**.

Igneous rock is rock formed from hot, melted, liquid material from deep inside the earth. Igneous rock is formed deep inside the earth and moves upward toward the earth's surface. An example of this liquid material is the lava that erupts from a volcano. When the lava reaches the surface of the earth, it cools and forms a hard, heavy, crystal-like rock called igneous rock. **Geologists**, scientists who study earth forms, believe that igneous rock makes up about 95 percent of the earth's outside layer. In some places, this igneous rock is nearly 40 miles thick (60 kilometers)!

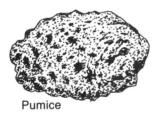

Pumice

Obsidian

Pumice is a gray or white rock. It is filled with small air spaces. It can float in the water. It is softer igneous rock and looks like a sponge.

Obsidian is very black and shiny. Sometimes it is called volcanic glass.

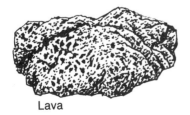

Lava

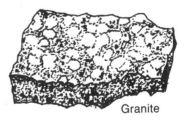

Granite

Lava is dark gray, brown, or black. It is filled with large air spaces. It does not float in water. It cools and hardens above the ground.

Granite has large crystals of minerals in it. It is a light-colored rock. It cools and hardens underground.

Sedimentary rock is soft rock. It is usually formed from **sediment** which is made of small loose or broken parts of other rock and pieces of dead plants or animals. When the sediment hardens together, it forms sedimentary rock. Sedimentary rock and sediment cover three-fourths of the earth's land. This sediment and sedimentary rock is just a thin layer, like a skin over the land. Igneous and metamorphic rock just under the surface peek out through the sedimentary layer in many places.

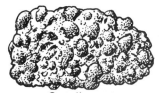
Conglomerate

A conglomerate is made of small rocks and sand. The small, rounded rocks are easy to see in the background of rough sand.

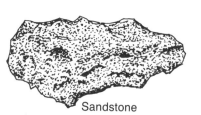
Sandstone

Sandstone is made from sand. The stone feels rough and is many different colors—red, brown, gray, yellow. If you put water on it, the water will soak into the stone.

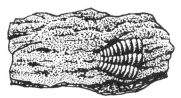
Limestone

Limestone is made up of shells and other material from the sea. It is either gray or white.

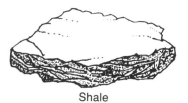
Shale

Shale is made from mud or clay. If you put water on shale, you can smell the earth or clay. It is a soft rock that is easily broken.

Metamorphic rock is rock that is under the surface of the earth, too. Metamorphic means changed. This kind of rock has been changed over a long time by heat or pressure or chemical reactions inside the earth. It is a very hard rock. Metamorphic rock was changed in its hard form. It was never a melted, hot liquid.

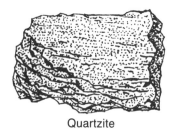
Quartzite

Quartzite is very hard. It has a glassy shine when it is first broken. Quartzite is metamorphosed sandstone.

Marble

Marble is a beautiful, pure white rock, but it sometimes has other colors mixed in—green, yellow, orange, brown, black. Marble is a metamorphosed limestone.

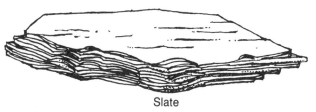
Slate

Slate has a smooth surface and cracks on the side. It is gray. Slate is a metamorphosed or changed shale.

The thirteen natural regions of the United States all have their own special features. They all have their own history of geologic processes, their own kinds of rock and rock structures, and different elevations. These different geologic histories shaped a wide variety of beautiful landscapes.

SELF-EVALUATION 4

VOCABULARY TICKETS

Read the vocabulary tickets with your teacher and the whole class. Are there still some words you do not understand? Write these words in a notebook. With a partner, write some example sentences using these new words. Talk about the meaning of these words with your classmates.

VOCABULARY CHECK

Here are some important words from this reading. Do you understand all of these words? Circle the words you do not understand. Then find the words in the reading. Talk about the meaning of these words with your classmates. If you know all the words, continue to the Question Review.

geologists	metamorphic rock	sedimentary rock
horizontally	rock structure	vertically
igneous rock	sediment	

QUESTION REVIEW

Go back to the questions on page 36. Look at your answers. Work with a partner. Look at your partner's answers too. Are they the same as your answers? Help each other write the correct answers.

CHAPTER REVIEW

Now that you have completed your reading about the landscape, go back to pages 22, 23, and 24. Look at your first ideas about the landscape. Have your ideas changed? What have you learned? Talk about your ideas with the teacher and the whole class.

EXTENSION ACTIVITIES

A. PLANNING A TRIP ACROSS THE COUNTRY

Materials

a road map of the United States for each group

LEARNING STRATEGY

☆ **Reading selectively**

With your partners, look at two maps. One map is on page 38. It shows the landforms, or features, of the different regions of the United States. Your teacher will give you the other map. This map is an ordinary road map of the United States. It shows the cities, state boundaries, major highways, lakes, rivers, and national parks.

You and your group members will plan a trip by car from San Francisco, California, to Boston, Massachusetts. You will leave San Francisco on July 10. You must be in Boston by September 10. You have two months to travel and you want to see as many different landscapes of the United States as you possibly can as you drive east.

1. Choose the areas you would like to visit.

2. Decide together with your group which cities or towns you will stay in.

3. Plan to drive no more than 200 miles in one day.

4. Stay in any area as long as you like.

5. Look for the roads and highways you will have to take.

6. Try to visit places that will give you a variety of landscapes, such as lakes, mountain areas, deserts, plateaus and beaches.

7. When you have decided on your itinerary (where you will go, by what roads, and for how long), write your itinerary on a chart like this:

Date	Route (Roads and Highways)	Destination (Where you will stay)	How many days?	Things to see

B. FIND THE FEATURES   Look at the diagram below. It shows the surface of a region and a cross section of the earth. With your partners, locate the features that you learned about in this chapter.

coastal plain	mountain range	valley
lake	lava	river
plain	canyon	creek
high plateau	eruption	vent

C. BUILD A VOLCANO!

Materials

a measuring cup	a cup of flour	vinegar
a spoon	water	a cup of salt
a pair of scissors	a piece of posterboard	a bowl
tape	a cardboard tube from	baking soda
red and green	a roll of toilet tissue	
food coloring		

1. Mix the flour and salt in a bowl.

2. Add cold water to the mixture slowly to make a dry, soft dough.

3. Add a few drops of red and green food coloring to the dough to turn it brown.

4. Cut a piece of the cardboard tube about three inches long.

5. Tape the piece of tube to the center of the posterboard to hold it in place. Seal the tube carefully where it is joined to the posterboard.

6. Pat the dough around the little tube and make it into the shape of a volcano. Pat the dough up and over the edge of the tube, but do not close the end of the tube.

7. Leave your volcano to get hard overnight.

8. The next day, put three tablespoons of baking soda into the "central vent" of your volcano. Add two or three drops of red food coloring.

9. Finally, pour in three tablespoons of vinegar. Watch your volcano "erupt"!

D. VOCABULARY REVIEW

Work with a partner. Fill in the vocabulary words from Chapter 2.

1. A long line of mountains _____

2. The geologic process that forms volcanoes

_____

3. A small lake _____

4. Wide, flat areas of land with high elevation

_____

5. Rock that is made up of small pieces of other rock and sand

_____

6. Rock formed by hot, liquid earth that has cooled

_____

7. A small river _____

8. A scientist who studies rocks and minerals

_____

9. The wearing away, or carrying away, of topsoil by water

_____

10. A volcanic explosion _____

11. A shallow valley or low place between mountains

_____

12. Metamorphic means _____

GLOSSARY

basin A shallow valley or low place between mountains.

canyon A deep valley with steep sides between two mountains.

coastal plain A large area of low, level land near the ocean.

creeks Natural streams of running water that are smaller than rivers.

drainage basin An area of small creeks and streams that run into larger rivers. Rain water is collected in drainage basins and carried to a large lake or ocean.

earthquakes Violent shaking or rolling of the earth; a geologic process.

elevation A measurement upwards from sea level.

erosion The wearing away, or carrying away, of the surface of the earth by wind or running water.

erupts Explodes; melted material and ash come out from a volcano.

features Parts of something.

geologic processes Natural movements or changes of the earth over time.

geologists Scientists who study rocks, minerals, and other earth formations.

horizontally Sideways, flat; parallel to the horizon.

igneous rock Rock formed from molten or melted earth material inside of the earth. When this liquid material cools, it hardens into crystal-like rock.

lake A large body of fresh or salt water smaller than a sea or ocean.

landscape All the natural features of a region looked at together form a landscape.

lava Liquid rock that erupts out onto the surface of the earth from a vent in a volcano. Inside the earth, it is called magma; outside on the surface of the earth, it is called lava.

magma Very hot, liquid rock containing gases and water found deep under the surface of the earth.

metamorphic rock Rock that has been changed into a different form by pressure and movement inside the earth.

mountain areas Landscape made up of high mountain peaks, shallow basins, and deep valleys.

natural regions Areas of the earth that are set apart naturally by their features, such as mountains, plains, or plateaus.

plains Large areas of flat, level land with no trees.

plateaus Large areas of flat, level land that are higher than the land that surrounds it; flat lands with a high elevation.

ponds Small lakes.

pressures Pushing or squeezing movements.

range A long line or chain of mountains.

rock structure The arrangement of rock, the position in which rock lies, such as a horizontal structure or a vertical structure.

running water Water that moves such as that in rivers and creeks.

sea level The level of the surface of the ocean.

sediment Small pieces of rock and sand found on the bottom of rivers, lakes, and streams and on the land.

sedimentary rock Soft rock that is made of small pieces of broken rock and sand which has become cemented together.

soil Broken down rock and organic material mixed together.

still water Water on the land that is not moving such as in lakes and ponds.

streams Any natural running water such as a creek or river.

topography The study of the surface of the earth and its different features and landscapes.

topsoil The top layer of dirt or soil that covers the earth. Plants grow in topsoil; erosion may remove topsoil.

uplift A geologic process that forms mountains by moving rock upward toward the surface.

valleys Low or deep areas between mountains.

vertically In a direction up and down.

volcanism The geologic process that forms volcanoes.

volcanoes Vents, or holes in the earth, through which lava and steam are thrown; mountains that form around the vents.

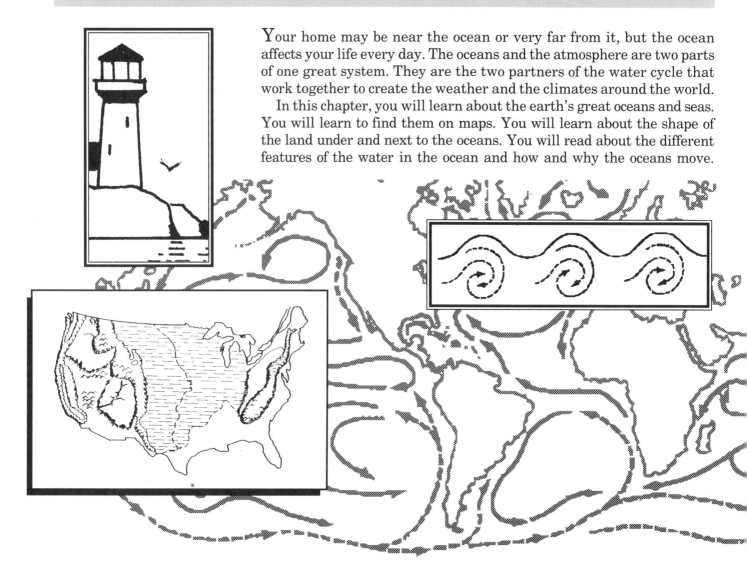

3 OCEANOGRAPHY
OCEANS AND SEAS

INTRODUCTION

Your home may be near the ocean or very far from it, but the ocean affects your life every day. The oceans and the atmosphere are two parts of one great system. They are the two partners of the water cycle that work together to create the weather and the climates around the world.

In this chapter, you will learn about the earth's great oceans and seas. You will learn to find them on maps. You will learn about the shape of the land under and next to the oceans. You will read about the different features of the water in the ocean and how and why the oceans move.

CRITICAL THINKING ACTIVITIES

WHAT DO YOU ALREADY KNOW ABOUT THE OCEANS AND SEAS?

LEARNING STRATEGIES
☆ Using prior knowledge ☆ Working cooperatively

Read the sentences. Draw a circle around the words you do not understand. Underline the words you cannot pronounce.

The oceans are the earth's largest bodies of water.
Ocean water is salty.
A sea is smaller than an ocean.
Many plants and animals live in the ocean.
Some parts of the ocean are shallow; some parts are deep.

Sit down with a partner. Look at your book and your partner's book. Help each other understand the words that are circled. Help each other pronounce the words that are underlined.

THINK ABOUT THESE IDEAS

LEARNING STRATEGIES
☆ Inferencing ☆ Working cooperatively ☆ Self-evaluation

Work in groups of three or four. Work together to answer these questions. If you are not sure about the answers, guess!

1. Remember what you learned about the weather in Chapter 1? How do you think the ocean and the atmosphere are connected? How do they work together to cause weather?
2. Some parts of the ocean are very salty. Other parts of the ocean, especially near land, are often less salty. What do you think causes an ocean to be very salty or less salty?
3. Some oceans are as warm as swimming pools. Other oceans are very cold. What do you think causes these different ocean temperatures?
4. In areas where the ocean is shallow, there are many plants and animals. In the very deep parts of the ocean, there are fewer living things. Why do you think this is true?

When your group finishes talking about these ideas, share your ideas with the whole class. Are your ideas different? Are they similar? After you read this chapter, look at these ideas and your answers again. Do not worry if your answers are right or wrong.

GROUP OBSERVATIONS

LEARNING STRATEGIES
☆ Grouping ☆ Interpreting data ☆ Self-evaluation

Work in groups of four.

1. The word **sea** is often used to mean the ocean. If we say that a man is going to sea, we mean that he is going out on the ocean. But the name *sea* is also given to small regions of the ocean that are partly surrounded by land. For example, the Sea of Cortez is a small part of the Pacific Ocean that is surrounded by Baja California and the mainland of Mexico. Look at the map on the next page. Find and read the names of seven different areas of ocean. Find and read the names of twenty seas.

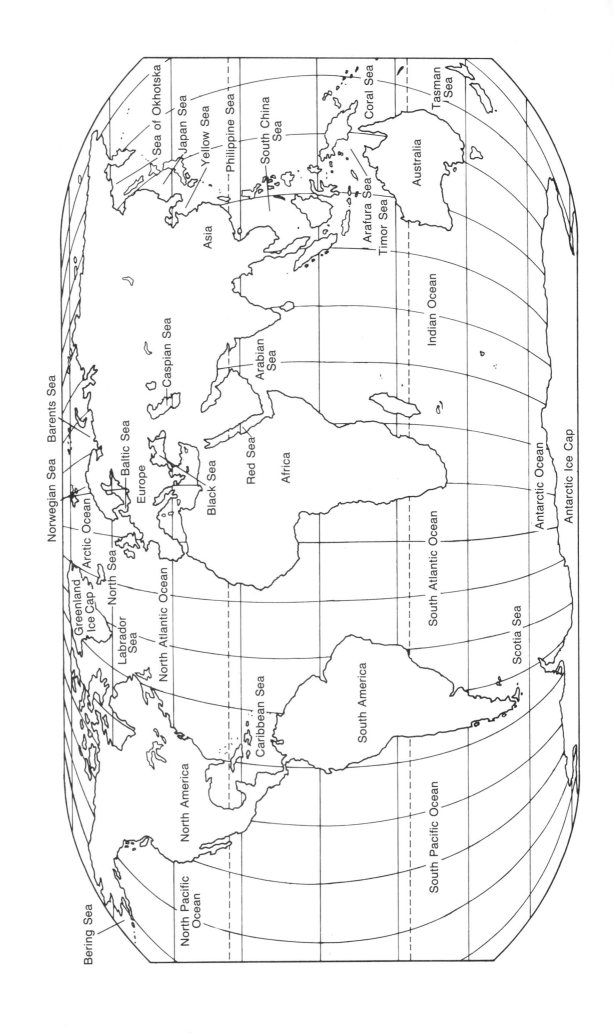

Sea of Okhotsk
Japan Sea
Yellow Sea
Philippine Sea
South China Sea
Coral Sea
Tasman Sea
Australia
Arafura Sea
Timor Sea
Asia
Caspian Sea
Arabian Sea
Indian Ocean
Norwegian Sea
Barents Sea
Baltic Sea
Europe
Black Sea
Red Sea
Africa
Greenland Ice Cap
Arctic Ocean
North Sea
North Atlantic Ocean
Labrador Sea
South Atlantic Ocean
Antarctic Ocean
Antarctic Ice Cap
Scotia Sea
North America
Caribbean Sea
South America
South Pacific Ocean
North Pacific Ocean
Bering Sea

2. With your partners, decide which oceans and seas are the **boundaries** for each continent. Some continents will have other continents as boundaries! Look at the example:

> Europe: north: Arctic Ocean
> south: Mediterranean Sea
> east: Asia
> west: Atlantic Ocean

Now, in your notebooks, do the same with Africa, North America, South America, Asia, and Australia.

3. *Materials*

> A relief map of the world

Your teacher will bring a relief map of the world.

Compare features on the land and under the oceans. Look for mountains, mountain ranges, and valleys on land and under the ocean. Write the names of some of these features and their location. Help your partners.

	On Land	**Under the Ocean**
Mountain name	_____	_____
Mountain location	_____	_____
Mountain range name	_____	_____
Mountain range location	_____	_____
Valley name	_____	_____
Valley location	_____	_____

4. Look at the table below. With your group members, answer the following questions.

   a. Which ocean is the deepest?
   b. Which ocean is the shallowest?
   c. How deep is the Indian Ocean at its deepest point?
   d. What is the surface area of the Arctic Ocean?
   e. Which ocean is the largest?

The Five Great Oceans

Ocean	Average depth (*in feet*)	Deepest point (*in feet*)	Surface area (*in square miles*)
Antarctic Ocean	12,240	21,038	12,352,000
Arctic Ocean	3,952	17,880	5,687,000
Atlantic Ocean	12,100	29,000	37,828,000
Indian Ocean	10,037	25,344	25,283,000
Pacific Ocean	13,355	36,200	63,690,000

5. Look at the list of the ten largest **islands** on earth. With your group members, decide how to put them in order from the biggest to the smallest. Write the names in order in your notebook.

The Ten Largest Islands

Island	Area (*in square miles*)	Location
Baffin	196,000	Arctic Ocean
Borneo	280,000	South Pacific Ocean
Ellesmere	75,000	Arctic Ocean
Great Britain	84,000	Atlantic Ocean
Greenland	840,000	North Atlantic Ocean
Honshu	88,000	Pacific Ocean
Madagascar	226,000	Indian Ocean
New Guinea	306,000	South Pacific Ocean
Sumatra	165,000	Indian Ocean
Victoria	83,900	Arctic Ocean

Share your answers with the whole class. After you finish reading this chapter, come back to these questions and observations and read them again. Are your answers the same?

PRE-READING 1

FOCUS QUESTION

Skim the reading on pages 49, 50, 51, and 52 to find the answer to the question below. Underline the answer in your book. Write the answer below.

■ *How much of the earth's surface is covered by oceans?*

_____

_____

DETAIL QUESTIONS

LEARNING STRATEGY
☆ **Reading selectively**

Read "The Great Oceans" on pages 49, 50, 51, and 52. Find the details. Underline the answers in your book. Write the answers below. As you read, write down on your vocabulary tickets any words you do not understand or cannot pronounce.

1. Name the five great oceans. _____

_____

2. What are the two zones of the ocean? _____

_____

3. Why do we know so little about the sea life in the oceanic zone?

_____

_____

4. Who studies the plants and animals that live in the oceans?

_____

_____

5. What three things do we measure to describe an ocean?

_____

_____

6. What are two causes of lower salinity in some parts of the ocean?

_____

_____

7. What determines the temperature of an ocean? _____

_____

READING 1 ★

The Great Oceans

People who live in the central part of a large continent may never see an ocean, but the oceans affect all people everywhere. About a third of the earth's surface is covered by land. Over two-thirds is covered by the water of the five great oceans: the Atlantic, the Pacific, the Indian, the Antarctic, and the Arctic. The map below shows the oceans divided

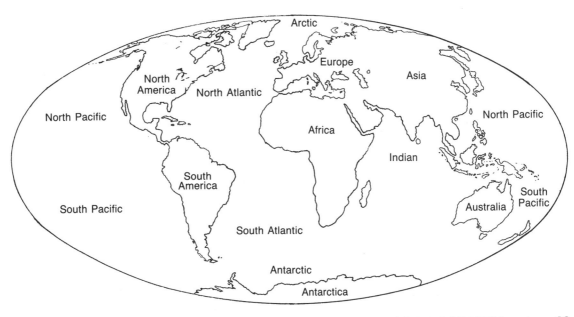

up into separate parts. In Chapter 1, we learned that all of the weather around the world is part of one large weather system. Similarly, the oceans in all areas of the world are part of one system, too.

The ocean floor, or bottom, is not flat and smooth. Under the ocean there are many mountains. Some of the earth's largest mountains are under the ocean. The largest range of mountains under the ocean is in the middle of the Atlantic. It runs north and south and is called the Mid-Atlantic Ridge. A **ridge** is a line of mountain tops or peaks along a mountain range. Some of the underwater mountains rise up so high that they form **islands**. Some islands are the peaks, or tops, of undersea mountains that rise up above sea level. Examples of these are the islands off the coast of Maine, Scotland, and the northwest coast of Spain. There are many volcanoes under the oceans, too. When the volcanoes are high enough to rise above the surface of the water, they form islands such as the Hawaiian Islands and many other islands in the South Pacific.

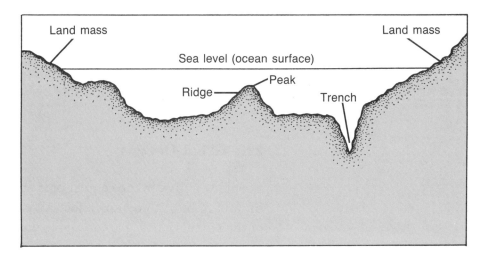

Under the ocean, there are also many deep valleys or **trenches**. Some of these trenches go down tens of thousands of feet. The deepest trenches are found in the South Pacific. For example, the Mariana Trench, shown to the right, has been measured to be 36,198 feet deep. That is almost seven miles deep!

The oceans are divided into two **zones**, or areas—a deep zone and a shallow zone. The water is shallow in the area next to land. This area is called the **neritic zone**. The neritic zone covers the **continental shelf**, or the edge of the continent that is under water. Because the water is shallow in the neritic zone, light from the sun can pass all the way through the water to the sea bottom. There are many kinds of plants and animals living in this zone. Scientists who are called **marine biologists** study the sea life. The neritic zone is an area that is easy to study, and marine biologists have learned many important things.

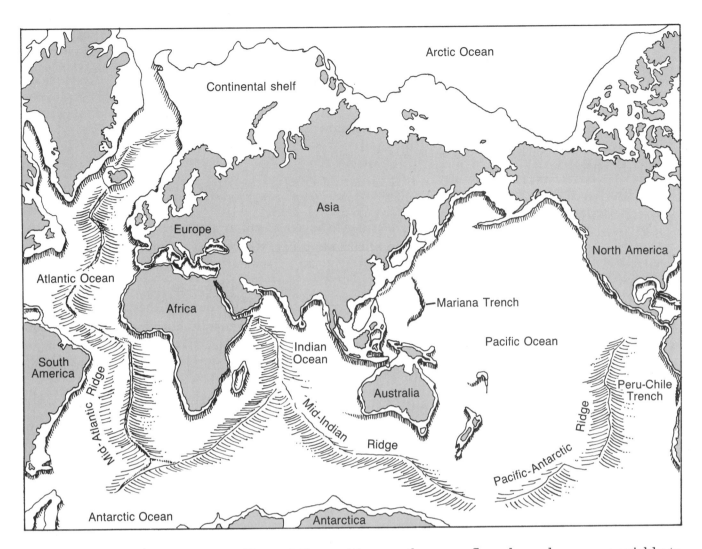

Beyond the neritic zone the ocean floor drops down very quickly to the main ocean bottom. This huge, deep area is called the **oceanic zone**. Fish live in the oceanic zone but not much is known about them. It is very difficult for marine biologists to study sea life in the oceanic zone because it is too dark and too deep. No plants live in the oceanic zone because there is no light.

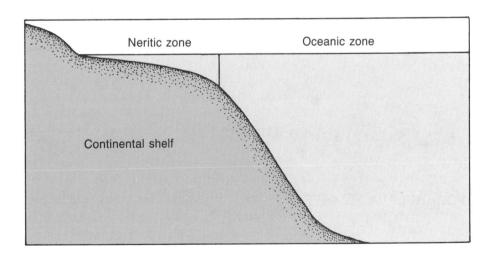

How are oceans different? How do oceans change? Oceans are measured by three things:

1. **salinity**, the amount of salt in the water
2. **temperature**, how warm or cold the water is
3. **depth**, how deep or shallow the water is

The salinity of the oceans is not the same everywhere. In deep water, the salinity changes very little. But next to the coast several things may cause the water to have less salt at times. Where a freshwater river runs into the ocean and mixes with the salt water, the ocean is less salty. (The salinity will be lower.) In polar regions, where ice is melting into the ocean, the water will have a lower salinity. And when there is heavy rainfall over the ocean, the ocean will have less salt.

Sometimes salinity will go up. For example, during a hot, dry summer, a lot of surface water in the ocean evaporates into the air. The water evaporates, but the salt does not. The salt is left behind, giving the water higher salinity.

The temperature of the ocean is determined by its latitude. Is the water near the poles or near the equator? It is also determined by how deep the water is and how warm or cool the air is over the water. Deep water in the polar regions is very cold. It may be cold enough to be covered with ice all year. Shallow water in a tropical area may be 86° Fahrenheit (30° centigrade). Shallow water is warmed by the sun, but the sun cannot reach the deep waters of the oceanic zone. When the air is warm over the ocean, such as off the coast of southern Mexico, the water temperature goes up. In the North Atlantic near Norway, the air is very cold. The water there is very cold, too.

The average depth of the ocean is about two miles (three kilometers). On the continental shelf and around islands, the water is shallow. In the oceanic zone, far away from land, the ocean may be seven miles deep.

The five great oceans of the world are not alike. There are many differences in depth, salinity, and temperature, but they are all part of one large water system. This system affects every living person on earth.

SELF-EVALUATION 1

VOCABULARY TICKETS

Read the vocabulary tickets with your teacher and the whole class. Are there still some words you do not understand? Write these words in a notebook. With a partner, write some example sentences using these new words. Talk about the meaning of these words with your classmates.

VOCABULARY CHECK

Here are some important words from this reading. Do you understand all of these words? Circle the words you do not understand. Then find the words in the reading. Talk about the meaning of these words with your classmates. If you know all the words, continue to the Question Review.

continental shelf	neritic zone	temperature
depth	oceanic zone	trenches
islands	ridge	zones
marine biologists	salinity	

QUESTION REVIEW

Go back to the questions on pages 48 and 49. Look at your answers. Work with a partner. Look at your partner's answers too. Are they the same as your answers? Help each other write the correct answers.

PRE-READING 2

FOCUS QUESTION

Skim the reading on pages 54, 55, 56, and 57 to find the answer to the question below. Underline the answer in your book. Write the answer below.

■ *What are three kinds of ocean movement?* _____

_____

DETAIL QUESTIONS

> **LEARNING STRATEGY**
>
> ☆ **Reading selectively**

Read "The Movement of the Oceans" on pages 54, 55, 56, and 57. Find the details. Underline the answers in your book. Write the answers below. As you read, write down on your vocabulary tickets any words you do not understand or cannot pronounce.

1. In which direction do tides pull the water in the ocean?

_____

_____

2. What causes tides? _____

_____

3. What causes waves? _____

_____

4. What are the three parts of a wave? _____

_____

5. In which direction do currents move? _____

_____

6. What shapes the currents? _____

_____

7. How do currents help to control the climate? _____

_____

The Movement of the Oceans

The ocean is always moving. It is never quiet. The ocean moves in **tides**, **waves**, and **currents**. Tides are the regular rise and fall of sea level once or twice a day. At high tide, ocean water moves in toward the land across a beach or a rocky **shore**. At low tide, it moves back out again. This movement is caused by the changing positions of the sun, the moon, and the earth.

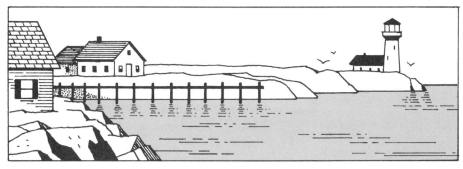

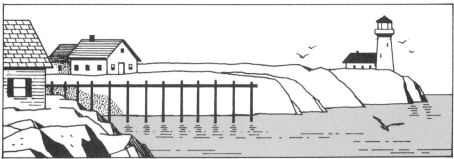

Cove at high and low tide

The movement of the tides is very complicated. There are many kinds of tides. In some parts of the world, tides move in and out only one time each day. In other places, there are tides two times a day. Some parts of the shore have irregular tides, tides that have no regular pattern.

Some coastlines have no tides! The differences in the movement of the tides are determined partly by the depth of the water and by the shape of the coastline. The movement of the tides changes the shape of the ocean floor and cleans the sand.

Waves are another kind of ocean movement. The winds that blow over the ocean make waves of all sizes. Hills and small mountains of water form in the ocean when the winds blow. The waves move in the same direction as the wind. When the wind stops, the waves smooth out a little, but they continue to move forward in the same direction.

The highest part of a wave is called the **crest**. The low area between two crests is called the **trough**. The distance between two wave crests is a **wavelength**. Large waves with very long wavelengths move quickly across the ocean. Smaller waves with very short wavelengths move much more slowly.

Waves change the temperature of the water. They stir and mix the warmer water on the surface with the colder water deep down.

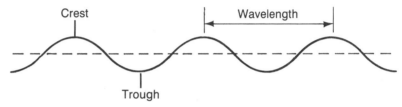

Parts of a wave

Large waves with long wavelengths move quickly.

Small waves with short wavelengths move slowly.

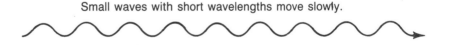

Waves mix surface water with water from deeper levels.

Winds blow in the same direction over the ocean for a long time. This unchanging wind pattern causes currents in the ocean. A current is like a river that moves through the ocean. These "rivers" carry very large amounts of water. Ocean currents usually move in the direction that the wind blows and they are shaped, or formed, by the land they move next to.

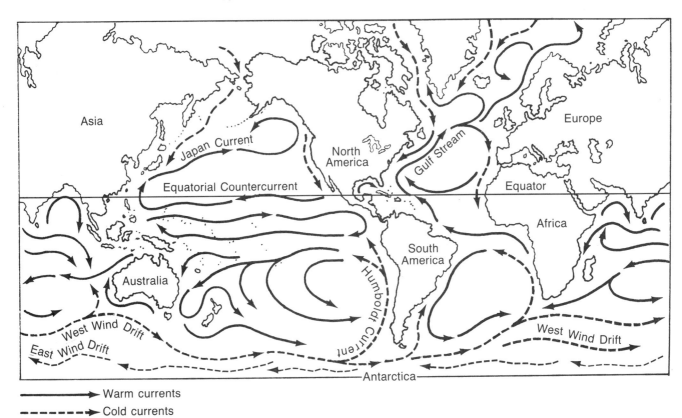

——————▶ Warm currents
- - - - - - ▶ Cold currents

Currents that begin near the equator carry warm water toward the colder water of the polar regions. Cold water in the polar regions is carried by currents to tropical areas. These currents mix the warm and cold waters.

Ocean currents affect climate all over the world. They help to control the temperature of the air. The Gulf Stream, for example, brings warm water from the Gulf of Mexico to the east coast of the United States and the lands of northwestern Europe. The Gulf Stream gives these areas a more comfortable, warmer climate than they would have without the ocean current.

The east coast of South America is warmed by water from the equator. The west coast of South America is cooled by the Humboldt Current. The west coast of the United States is cooled by the Japan Current.

Without ocean currents, air temperatures at the equator would be too high for humans to live there. Near the poles, air temperatures would be too low. Everything would be frozen solid. Ocean currents carry water back and forth around the earth moving heat and cold. They cool the air in the tropics and warm the air in the subarctic regions. Because there are ocean currents, people can live at all latitudes on the earth.

Tides are caused by the daily changing positions of the sun, moon, and earth. Waves and currents are caused by the winds around the earth. We are not able to control the movement of the ocean, but scientists hope to find ways to someday use the ocean as a source of energy.

SELF-EVALUATION 2

VOCABULARY TICKETS

Read the vocabulary tickets with your teacher and the whole class. Are there still some words you do not understand? Write these words in a notebook. With a partner, write some example sentences using these new words. Talk about the meaning of these words with your classmates.

VOCABULARY CHECK

Here are some important words from this reading. Do you understand all of these words? Circle the words you do not understand. Then find the words in the reading. Talk about the meaning of these words with your classmates. If you know all the words, continue to the Question Review.

crest	trough
currents	wavelength
shore	waves
tides	

QUESTION REVIEW

Go back to the questions on pages 53 and 54. Look at your answers. Work with a partner. Look at your partner's answers too. Are they the same as your answers? Help each other write the correct answers.

PRE-READING 3

FOCUS QUESTION

Skim the reading on pages 58, 59, and 60 to find the answer to the question below. Underline the answer in your book. Write the answer below.

■ *What are four different kinds of land you can find on a*

coastline? _____

_____

DETAIL QUESTIONS

LEARNING STRATEGY
☆ **Reading selectively**

Read "The Coastline: Where the Ocean Meets the Land" on pages 58, 59, and 60. Find the details. Underline the answers in your book. Write the answers below. As you read, write down on your vocabulary tickets any words you do not understand or cannot pronounce.

1. What is an estuary? _____

   _____

2. What kind of water is found in an estuary? _____

   _____

3. How is a swamp different from a marsh? _____

   _____

4. What is special about a mangrove tree? _____

   _____

5. What is special about intertidal animals and plants? _____

   _____

6. How do intertidal animals on the rocky shores protect themselves

   when the tide goes out? _____

   _____

7. How do intertidal animals on sandy beaches protect themselves

   when the tide goes out? _____

   _____

READING 3 ★

The Coastline: Where the Ocean Meets the Land

Land that is next to the ocean has many different forms. Along some coastlines, the ocean rolls gently onto long, narrow beaches such as on the Gulf of Mexico. In other places, such as Louisiana, ocean water meets and mixes with fresh water from a river in an area called an **estuary**. Along the coast of California the ocean often hits up against high **cliffs** or splashes over low, rocky shores. Along the coastline only very special plants and animals can live because their **environment** is constantly changing.

An estuary is a region where fresh water from a river mixes with ocean salt water that comes in with the high tide. This mixture of fresh and salt water is called **brackish water**. The high tide usually floods, or covers over, the land of the estuary once or twice a day.

The land in many estuaries is soft, wet, and muddy, and is under water part or all of the time. This land may be either a **marsh** or a **swamp**. In a marsh, many tall grasses grow. It is an area full of fish and other wildlife. Marshes serve as the "nursery grounds" of most of the fish that are commercially caught in the southeastern part of the United states. **Fisheries** of oysters, clams, and eels are often located in marshes.

Swamps are similar to marshes. But in swamps are thousands of **mangrove** trees that have replaced the tall grasses. Mangroves are very special trees that can live with their roots under water.

Some of the plants in the swamps or marshes of an estuary are under this brackish water all of the time, for example, eelgrass. Other plants, such as cordgrass, grow in the wet, salty soil that is covered by water only part of the day. The thick plants and trees that grow in an estuary give protection and food for thousands of birds, ducks, rats, turtles, and other animals.

Estuaries protect fish and other underwater animals from the pounding movement of the waters and currents. They also find plenty of food. Only certain sea animals can live in an estuary. They have to be able to live in both salt water and fresh water. Only a few kinds of oysters, clams, crabs, shrimp, and fish have bodies that can live in both kinds of water.

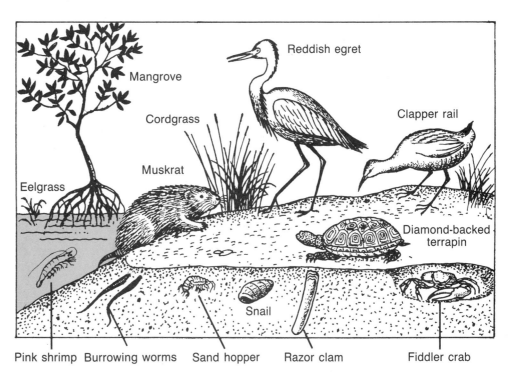

In addition to being the home of much wildlife and a center for fisheries, many large estuary regions serve as ports for other ocean businesses such as shipping and canning.

Intertidal plants and animals live along rocky shores and sandy beaches. Intertidal plants and animals can live both under the water and out in the air. For part of the day, when the tide is in, the plants and animals are covered with seawater. When the tide goes out again, it leaves plants and animals out on the rocks or in the mud or sand.

On rocky shores, plants, such as **seaweed**, attach themselves to the rocks with special parts like fingers. These plants hold water so that they stay moist when the tide is out. Their top parts may dry out, but the bottom of the plant stays wet and cool. Many small animals hide under the seaweed to protect themselves from the sun and wind. Some animals also hide in the cracks of dark, cool rocks. Animals with shells attach themselves to the rocks, too. When the water goes out with the tide, they hold onto the rocks, cover themselves tightly with their shells, and hold in some salt water. Then they wait for the tide to come back in to bring them food and water.

On the beaches waves break and roll over the sand many times each minute. The action of the waves moves the sand around and makes it difficult for plants to attach themselves. However, many animals live under the sand where the waves break. When the tide is out, most beach animals, such as clams, worms, and small crabs, hide under the soft, wet sand. Some of these animals eat dead fish or small pieces of seaweed carried up onto the beach by the waves. Many shorebirds run along the sand and dig down into the sand looking for the worms, crabs, and clams to eat.

Most of you have walked on sandy beaches or seen pictures of them. But not all beaches are covered with sand. Some beaches are made up of tiny rocks or small, smooth, flat stones. Along the coast of Alaska, beaches are often covered with large (3 inches to 8 inches) round stones.

All oceans are not the same. All coastlines are not the same, but all are interesting to study and beautiful to visit.

SELF-EVALUATION 3

VOCABULARY TICKETS

Read the vocabulary tickets with your teacher and the whole class. Are there still some words you do not understand? Write these words in a notebook. With a partner, write some example sentences using these new words. Talk about the meaning of these words with your classmates.

VOCABULARY CHECK

Here are some important words from this reading. Do you understand all of these words? Circle the words you do not understand. Then find the words in the reading. Talk about the meaning of these words with your classmates. If you know all the words, continue to the Question Review.

brackish water	intertidal
cliffs	mangrove
environment	marsh
estuary	seaweed
fisheries	swamp

QUESTION REVIEW

Go back to the questions on pages 57 and 58. Look at your answers. Work with a partner. Look at your partner's answers too. Are they the same as your answers? Help each other write the correct answers.

CHAPTER REVIEW

Now that you have completed your reading about the oceans and seas, go back to pages 45, 46, 47, and 48. Look at your first ideas about oceans and seas. Have your ideas changed? What have you learned? Talk about your ideas with the teacher and the whole class.

EXTENSION ACTIVITIES

A. OCEAN CURRENTS AND SALINITY

LEARNING STRATEGIES

☆ Inferencing
☆ Taking notes

Materials

1 box of table salt	2 glasses
2 different colors of ink	water
a glass jar with a wide top	measuring spoons

1. Dissolve a half a teaspoon of salt in a glass of water.
2. Color the water with a few drops of one color of ink.
3. Pour this mixture into the glass jar.
4. In another glass, dissolve four teaspoons of salt.
5. Color the water with a few drops of the other color of ink.
6. Slowly pour the very salty water into the jar with the less salty water.
7. Observe what happens with the water with the higher salinity. Does it mix easily with the other water? Does it stay on top or go to the bottom? Write some notes about what you observe.
8. Let the water stand in the jar for a few minutes. Do not touch or move the jar. What does the water look like after a few minutes? Are the waters completely mixed? Where in the ocean would you expect to find the water with the highest salinity: at the surface or on the bottom? Why?

B. OCEAN MOVEMENT AND WIND

LEARNING STRATEGIES

☆ Inferencing
☆ Taking notes

Materials

a large baking dish or pan	a hair dryer
a bottle of ink	warm and cold water
a piece of cardboard	ice cubes

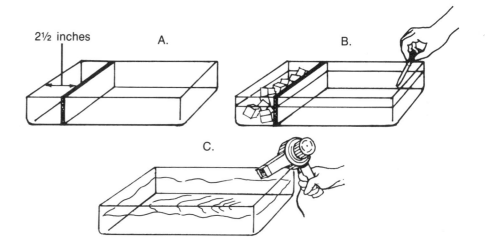

1. Cut a cardboard strip to fit the pan as you see in the illustration. It should fit tightly.

2. Place the cardboard strip in the pan about 2½ inches from one end. You will have one small section and one large section.

3. Pour warm water into the pan in both sections. The water should be a little over halfway to the top of the pan.

4. Fill the small section of the pan with ice cubes and wait until the water stops moving.

5. Add one or two drops of ink to the water on the side farthest away from the ice cubes.

6. Look at the water. What happens to the ink? Write some notes about what you observe. Talk with other students about why you think this happens.

7. Now, remove the cardboard strip and empty out the pan. Pour clean water into the pan again a little over halfway to the top of the pan. Let the water stand a minute to become still.

8. With a dropper, add one drop of ink to the bottom-center of the pan. Do not move the water as you do this.

9. Turn on the hair dryer to "high." Direct a stream of air across the surface of the water so that it makes small waves.

Observe the water. Watch what happens to the drop of ink. Write notes about what you see. Talk with other students about why you think this happens. Talk about your observations with a group of students. Try to answer these questions.

1. How does temperature affect the movement of ocean water?

2. How does wind affect the movement of ocean water?

C. CHARTING THE SEAS

Sit down in groups of four. Your teacher will give each group some large chart paper and some colored pens or pencils. Each group will choose one geographic area such as North America, South America, Africa, India, Antarctica, Europe, Asia, British Isles, or Southeast Asia. On your chart paper, map out this geographical area, including the oceans and seas that surround it, inland seas, and very large rivers that run into the sea. Be sure to label all of these water areas.

Hang these charts on the bulletin boards. Make them as interesting and as artistic as possible. Have the class vote on the chart they find most interesting. Give a prize. Share these charts with other classes when you are finished with your chapter.

D. WAVES, CURRENTS, AND TIDES

Sit down in groups of four. Go back and look at the charts and diagrams on pages 54, 55, and 56. Your teacher will give each group some large chart paper and some colored pens or pencils. Each group will choose one sea movement to illustrate. For example, one group will illustrate the movement of waves, and another group will chart out the major currents. Use the drawings in the chapter as models if you like, or create your own style of diagram. Label your chart.

Work together to write a paragraph or two that describes, or explains, what is in your drawing. Hang these charts on the bulletin boards. When you finish the chapter on the oceans and seas, share your charts with other classes.

E. VOCABULARY REVIEW

Work in groups. Fill in the vocabulary words from Chapter 3.

1. The movement of water away from the shore and in toward the shore is the _____.

2. The bottom of the ocean is its _____.

3. A small body of land that is completely surrounded by water is an _____.

4. What is the opposite of deep? _____

5. Small hills of water that form on the surface of the ocean are called _____.

6. The Mid-Atlantic _____ is a range of mountains under the ocean.

7. A river under the ocean is a _____.

8. The highest part of a wave is a _____.

9. The distances between crests of waves are called _____ _____.

10. The neritic zone lies above the continental _____.

11. The deep part of the ocean is called the _____ zone.

12. A measurement of how much salt is in the water is called _____.

GLOSSARY

boundaries Things that show the beginning or end of a place.

brackish water A mixture of salt water and fresh water found in estuaries.

cliffs High walls of rock on the coastline that drop down to meet the sea.

continental shelf The shallow part of the ocean that borders the continents.

crest The highest part of a wave.

currents Water that moves like a river under the surface of the ocean.

depth A measurement of how deep or shallow a body of water is.

environment The things and conditions around a living thing.

estuary A part of the coastline where ocean water meets fresh water from a river.

fisheries Businesses that catch, process, and sell fish.

intertidal Living in the tide zone, such as intertidal plants.

islands Land masses that are completely surrounded by water.

mangrove A kind of tree that lives in swamps; a tree that can live with its roots under water.

marine biologists Scientists who study plant and animal life under the sea.

marsh Wet, soft, muddy land covered with tall grasses and flooded with water; often found in estuaries.

neritic zone The shallow part of the ocean that covers the continental shelf, the area of water along the land.

oceanic zone The deep part of the ocean, far away from the shore.

ridge A line of mountain tops or peaks along a mountain range.

salinity The measurement of the amount of salt in a body of water.

sea A large body of water, smaller than an ocean, that is usually surrounded or nearly surrounded by land.

seaweed A type of plant that grows in the ocean or in the tide zone.

shore The land at the edge of a sea, ocean, lake, or river.

swamp Soft, wet, muddy land covered with water part or all of the time; a place where mangrove trees grow.

temperature The amount of heat or cold something has.

tides Movement of the ocean away from the shore and back toward the shore caused by the changing positions of the sun, the moon, and the earth.

trenches Large, deep valleys or cracks in the floor of the ocean.

trough The valley, or low place, between two wave crests.

wavelength The distance between two wave crests.

waves Hills of water that form when strong winds blow over the surface of the ocean.

zones Regions, parts of larger areas.

CHAPTER

4 PHYSICS AND CHEMISTRY

MATTER, MASS, AND MOLECULES

INTRODUCTION

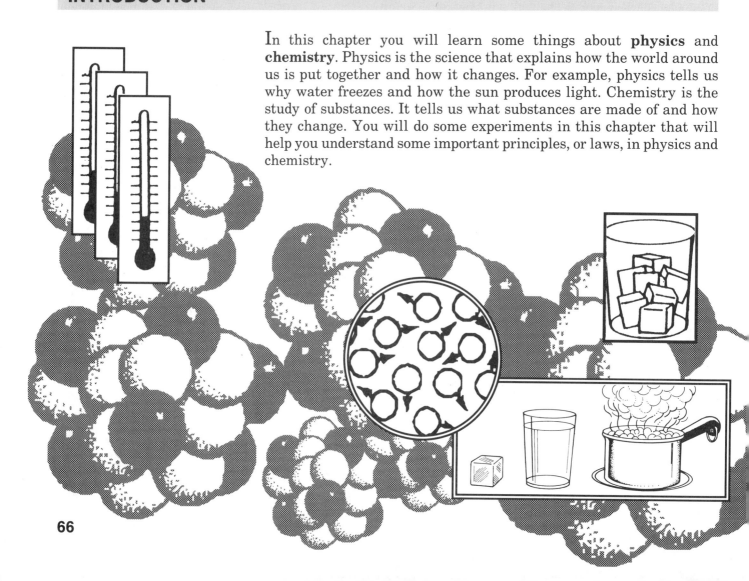

In this chapter you will learn some things about **physics** and **chemistry**. Physics is the science that explains how the world around us is put together and how it changes. For example, physics tells us why water freezes and how the sun produces light. Chemistry is the study of substances. It tells us what substances are made of and how they change. You will do some experiments in this chapter that will help you understand some important principles, or laws, in physics and chemistry.

CRITICAL THINKING ACTIVITIES

WHAT DO YOU ALREADY KNOW ABOUT PHYSICS AND CHEMISTRY?

LEARNING STRATEGIES
☆ Using prior knowledge
☆ Working cooperatively

Read these sentences. Draw a circle around the words you do not understand. Underline the words you cannot pronounce.

Air contains oxygen.

Molecules are very small.

People weigh less on the moon.

Ice becomes water when it is heated.

Most cooking pots and pans have wooden or plastic handles.

Sit down with a partner. Look at your book and your partner's book. Help each other understand the words that are circled. Help each other pronounce the words that are underlined.

THINK ABOUT THESE IDEAS

LEARNING STRATEGIES
☆ Working cooperatively
☆ Sequencing
☆ Self-evaluation

Work in groups of three or four. Work together to answer these questions. If you are not sure about the answers, guess!

1. With your group, look at the following pictures carefully. Read what is in each cup. Decide which cup is the lightest. Mark it number 1. Which cup is the heaviest? Mark it number 6. Mark the other four cups in order of their weight. Talk about this in your group.

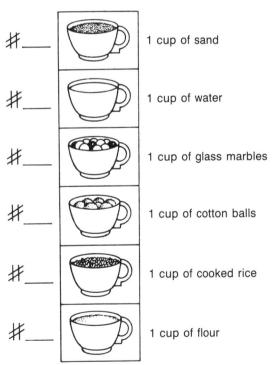

\# ___   1 cup of sand

\# ___   1 cup of water

\# ___   1 cup of glass marbles

\# ___   1 cup of cotton balls

\# ___   1 cup of cooked rice

\# ___   1 cup of flour

In what order did your group put the cups? Why do some cups weigh more than other cups?

2. What are the handles on pots and pans generally made of? Why?

3. With your group, try to make a list of all the different things that you would need to make one of the following foods: chocolate cake, sugar cookies, spaghetti sauce. Then, decide how much of each thing you will need. Be prepared to share your answers with the whole class.

When your group finishes talking about these ideas, share your ideas with the whole class. Are your ideas different? Are they similar? After you read this chapter, look at these ideas and your answers again. Do not worry if your answers are right or wrong.

GROUP OBSERVATIONS

LEARNING STRATEGIES
☆ **Taking notes**
☆ **Sequencing**
☆ **Inferencing**

Materials

eyedropper	ice cubes
sugar	ink
glass jar	hot plate or other heating instrument

1. Fill a glass jar with water. Fill an eyedropper with a little ink. Put three or four drops of ink in the water. Watch what happens to the ink and the water. Then discuss what happened.

   a. Scientists have to keep records of their experiments. Imagine you are a scientist. In your notebook, explain step by step how your group conducted this activity. Use the words *first, second, next, then,* and *finally* in explaining the process your group went through. Be prepared to share your work with the whole class.

   b. Why did this happen to the ink and water? Give your hypothesis, or best guess, based on what you saw and what you know.

2. Fill a glass jar with water. Add two teaspoons of sugar to the water. Watch what happens to the water. Stir the water. Taste the water. Discuss what happened with your group.

   a. Scientists have to record their experiments. Imagine you are a scientist. In your notebook, explain step by step how your group conducted this activity.

   b. Why did this happen to the sugar and water? Write down your hypothesis.

3. Your teacher will put three or four ice cubes in a pan on a hot plate, in an electric frying pan, or a coffee pot and turn it on high. Watch what happens to the ice cubes. Discuss what happened with your group.

   a. Scientists have to record their experiments. Imagine you are a scientist. In your notebook, explain step by step how your group conducted this activity. Be prepared to share your work with the entire group.

   b. Why did these things happen? Write down your hypothesis.

Share your answers with the whole class. After you finish reading this chapter, come back to these questions and observations and read them again. Are your answers the same?

PRE-READING 1

FOCUS QUESTION

Skim the reading on pages 70, 71, and 72 to find the answer to the question below. Underline the answer in your book. Write the answer below.

■ *What is everything on the earth made up of?* _____

_____

DETAIL QUESTIONS

LEARNING STRATEGY
☆ **Reading selectively**

Read "Recipes from the Earth" on pages 70, 71, and 72. Find the details. Underline the answers in your book. Write the answers below. As you read, write down on your vocabulary tickets any words you do not understand or cannot pronounce.

1. What are elements? _____

_____

2. How many different elements are there? _____

_____

3. Name one of the most common elements. _____

_____

4. What is matter? _____

_____

5. What are molecules made of? _____

_____

6. What are pure elements? _____

_____

7. What is a compound? _____

_____

Recipes from the Earth

Have you ever made cookies or helped someone else make cookies? If you have, you know that there are steps you need to follow. One step is putting all the **ingredients** into a bowl. Ingredients are the separate things you need to make something. The ingredients for cookies are such things as milk, eggs, flour, butter, salt, and sugar. When all of these separate things are mixed together in the right amounts and baked in the oven, you have cookies. Remember this idea when you study the information in this chapter.

The earth and everything on the earth is also made up of ingredients. Each ingredient is called an **element**. Everything in the world is made of elements that are mixed, or combined together, in different ways. The earth, the air, and the water are made up of elements. There are 109 different elements. There are 92 elements which occur naturally in the world and 17 more that scientists have made.

The table that follows lists the 109 different elements. Each element has a **symbol** that uses only one or two letters from the Latin name. For example, the symbol for oxygen is O. Each element also has a number. The number for oxygen is 8. Study the table and try to remember some of the elements. It is not necessary to memorize all 109 elements now. Did you know some of the elements before you saw this table? If yes, how many? Which ones?

Some of the ingredients for making cookies are sugar, milk, flour, and eggs. Some of the ingredients that make up the earth are **oxygen**, **carbon**, and **hydrogen**. One of the most common elements is oxygen. It can be found everywhere. Oxygen makes up about a fifth of the air we breathe.

The study of all the ingredients or elements that make up the earth is called **chemistry**. When you put all the ingredients for cookies together in a bowl and mix them up, you have a batter. When elements from the earth are combined, it is **matter**. Matter is anything that takes up space. For example, water is matter. Your desk is matter. Matter is made up of different elements. The elements that make up water are hydrogen and oxygen. The elements that make up your desk are very different.

The smallest **particle** of an element is called an **atom**. Atoms may combine to form a **molecule**. Molecules cannot be seen with the **naked eye**. Some molecules, like oxygen, hydrogen, and **chlorine** molecules are made up of only one kind of atom. **Pure elements** are made up of only one kind of atom. Some molecules like water and

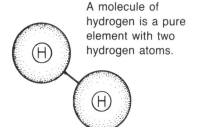

A molecule of hydrogen is a pure element with two hydrogen atoms.

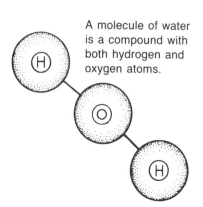

A molecule of water is a compound with both hydrogen and oxygen atoms.

Pure elements are made up of only one kind of atom. Compounds are molecules with different kinds of atoms.

Table of the Elements

Name	Symbol	No.	Name	Symbol	No.
Actinium	Ac	89	Mercury	Hg	80
Aluminium	Al	13	Molybdenum	Mo	42
Americium	Am	95	Neodymium	Nd	60
Antimony	Sb	51	Neon	Ne	10
Argon	Ar	18	Neptunium	Np	93
Arsenic	As	33	Nickel	Ni	28
Astatine	At	85	Niobium	Nb	41
Barium	Ba	56	Nitrogen	N	7
Berkelium	Bk	97	Nobelium	No	102
Beryllium	Be	4	Osmium	Os	76
Bismuth	Bi	83	Oxygen	O	8
Boron	B	5	Palladium	Pd	46
Bromine	Br	35	Phosphorus	P	15
Cadmium	Cd	48	Platinum	Pt	78
Caesium	Cs	55	Plutonium	Pu	94
Calcium	Ca	20	Polonium	Po	84
Californium	Cf	98	Potassium	K	19
Carbon	C	6	Praesodymium	Pr	59
Cerium	Ce	58	Promethium	Pm	61
Chlorine	Cl	17	Protactinium	Pa	91
Chromium	Cr	24	Radium	Ra	88
Cobalt	Co	27	Radon	Rn	86
Copper	Cu	29	Rhenium	Re	75
Curium	Cm	96	Rhodium	Rh	45
Dysprosium	Dy	66	Rubidium	Rb	37
Einsteinium	Es	99	Ruthenium	Ru	44
Erbium	Er	68	Samarium	Sm	62
Europium	Eu	63	Scandium	Sc	21
Fermium	Fm	100	Selenium	Se	34
Fluorine	F	9	Silicon	Si	14
Francium	Fr	87	Silver	Ag	47
Gadolinium	Gd	64	Sodium	Na	11
Gallium	Ga	31	Strontium	Sr	38
Germanium	Ge	32	Sulphur	S	16
Gold	Au	79	Tantalum	Ta	73
Hafnium	Hf	72	Technetium	Tc	43
Helium	He	2	Tellurium	Te	52
Holmium	Ho	67	Terbium	Tb	65
Hydrogen	H	1	Thallium	Tl	81
Indium	In	49	Thorium	Th	90
Iodine	I	53	Thulium	Tm	69
Iridium	Ir	77	Tin	Sn	50
Iron	Fe	26	Titanium	Ti	22
Krypton	Kr	36	Tungsten (Wolfram)	W	74
Lanthanum	La	57	Uranium	U	92
Lawrencium	Lr	103	Vanadium	V	23
Lead	Pb	82	Xenon	Xe	54
Lithium	Li	3	Ytterbium	Yb	70
Lutetium	Lu	71	Yttrium	Y	39
Magnesium	Mg	12	Zinc	Zn	30
Manganese	Mn	25	Zirconium	Zr	40
Mendelevium	Md	101			

Elements 104, 105, 106 and 107 have been discovered by Russian and American scientists, but names have not yet been agreed for them. The Americans call elements 104 and 105 rutherfordium and hahnium, but the Russians call them kurchatovium and nielsbohrium.

sugar are made of different kinds of atoms. When two or more different kinds of atoms combine, the new unit is called a **compound**.

In this reading you learned some beginning concepts in chemistry. You learned about the ingredients that make up everything in the world around us. These ingredients are called elements. You also learned that when these elements are put together, it is matter. In the next reading, you will learn more about matter and the rules that govern it.

SELF-EVALUATION 1

VOCABULARY TICKETS

Read the vocabulary tickets with your teacher and the whole class. Are there still some words you do not understand? Write these words in a notebook. With a partner, write some example sentences using these new words. Talk about the meaning of these words with your classmates.

VOCABULARY CHECK

Here are some important words from this reading. Do you understand all of these words? Circle the words you do not understand. Then find the words in the reading. Talk about the meaning of these words with your classmates. If you know all the words, continue to the Question Review.

atom	element	naked eye
carbon	hydrogen	oxygen
chemistry	ingredients	particle
chlorine	matter	pure element
compound	molecule	symbol

QUESTION REVIEW

Go back to the questions on page 69. Look at your answers. Work with a partner. Look at your partner's answers too. Are they the same as your answers? Help each other write the correct answers.

PRE-READING 2

FOCUS QUESTION

Skim the reading on pages 73, 74, and 75 to find the answer to the question below. Underline the answer in your book. Write the answer below.

■ *What three things do scientists define when they describe*

matter? _____

_____

Read "Mass and Matter" on pages 73, 74, and 75. Find the details. Underline the answers in your book. Write the answers below. As you read, write down on your vocabulary tickets any words you do not understand or cannot pronounce.

LEARNING STRATEGY
☆ **Reading selectively**

1. What is the difference between weight and mass? _____

   _____

2. Does a 200-pound man weigh more or less than 200 pounds on

   the moon? _____

   _____

3. What are the three basic states of matter? _____

   _____

4. Finish these sentences: When the molecules in water are close

   together and moving very slowly, water is in a _____

   state. When the molecules are moving very fast and are very far

   apart, water is in a _____ state.

5. Explain what heat does to molecules. _____

   _____

READING 2 ★

Mass and Matter

When scientists describe matter they define its **mass**, its **weight**, and its **state**, or form. The amount of matter in an object is called mass. For example, a car, a tricycle, and a house all have mass. A car has a greater mass than a tricycle; a house has a greater mass than a car. Mass is not the same as weight. Weight is caused by the pull of **gravity** on an object. Gravity is a force or pull toward an object. Mass does not change, but weight can change depending on how far from the earth an object is. Mass stays the same whether it is on Earth, the moon, or in deep space. For example, the moon has only one-sixth the gravity of Earth. Your mass on the moon would be the same as your mass on Earth, but your weight would be only one-sixth of what you weigh on Earth. The pull, or force of gravity on the moon is less than it is on the Earth. If you can jump 3 feet on Earth, you can jump 18 feet on the moon. An **astronaut** must wear special clothing on the moon because he or she weighs less. But astronauts have the same mass on the moon as they do on the Earth.

A game of catch on the moon with only one-sixth the gravity of Earth

Matter comes in three states, or forms. These three states are **solid**, **liquid**, and **gas**. Ice is matter in a solid state. When the ice melts, it is water. Water is a liquid state. When the water gets very hot, it turns to **water vapor**. Water vapor is a gas, or the **gaseous** state of water.

THE THREE STATES OF WATER

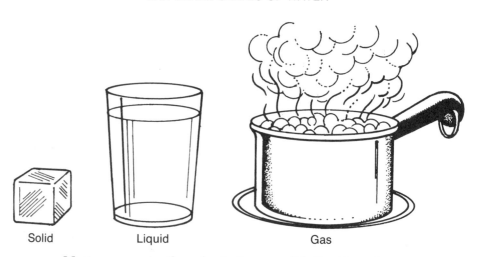

Solid   Liquid   Gas

Matter comes in three basic forms: solid, liquid, and gas.

The molecules move at different speeds in the three states of matter. For example, when the molecules in water are close together and move very slowly, the water is in a solid state. It is ice. When the molecules speed up and move away from each other, water is in a liquid state.

When the molecules move very fast and are very far apart, water is in a gaseous state. It is water vapor. Heat causes molecules to speed up and begin moving away from each other.

MOLECULES IN THE THREE STATES OF MATTER

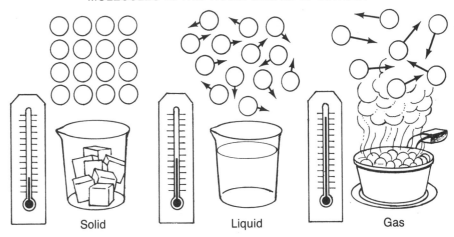

Solid   Liquid   Gas

In this reading you learned three important things about matter. You also learned about the mass and weight of matter. You learned about the three states of matter. In the next reading, you will continue learning about matter and other ways to talk about differences in matter.

SELF-EVALUATION 2

VOCABULARY TICKETS

Read the vocabulary tickets with your teacher and the whole class. Are there still some words you do not understand? Write these words in a notebook. With a partner, write some example sentences using these new words. Talk about the meaning of these words with your classmates.

VOCABULARY CHECK

Here are some important words from this reading. Do you understand all of these words? Circle the words you do not understand. Then find the words in the reading. Talk about the meaning of these words with your classmates. If you know all the words, continue to the Question Review.

astronaut	mass
gas	solid
gaseous	state
gravity	water vapor
liquid	weight

PRE-READING 3

FOCUS QUESTION

Skim the reading on pages 76 and 77 to find the answer to the question below. Underline the answer in the reading. Write the answer below.

■ *What are two ways to talk about the differences in matter?*

_____

_____

DETAIL QUESTIONS

LEARNING STRATEGY
☆ **Reading selectively**

Read "Properties of Matter" on pages 76 and 77. Find the details. Underline the answers in your book. Write the answers below. As you read, write down on your vocabulary tickets any words you do not understand or cannot pronounce.

1. What are three properties of matter? _____

_____

2. Which has a greater density, a cup of cotton balls or a cup of glass

    marbles? _____

_____

3. Which is a better conductor of heat, wood or metal? _____

_____

READING 3 ★

Properties of Matter

We can talk about the differences in matter in two ways: by naming the differences in the elements that make up matter and by describing the **properties** of matter. For example, water is different from salt because it is made up of different elements. Water is made of oxygen and hydrogen while salt is made of **sodium** and chlorine. Matter also has different properties such as its color, odor, and taste, a freezing point, and a boiling point. For example, sugar and salt taste different, salt and pepper smell different and have a different color. In this reading, you will learn about three other properties of matter: **density**, **solubility**, and **conductivity**.

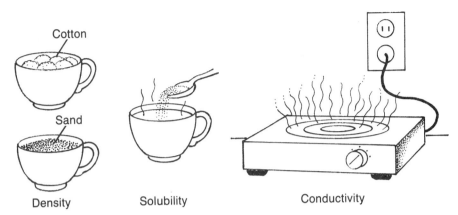

Three properties of matter that are important for scientists to know about are density, solubility, and conductivity.

Density is how much matter you can put into a certain space. In the activities at the beginning of this chapter, you looked at six different cups with different matter in each cup. Some cups were heavy and some were light. This is because the density of the matter in the cups was different. The tiny elements that make up glass marbles are much closer and tighter together than the elements that make up the cotton balls. The matter of the glass marbles has more density.

Solubility is the ability of matter to **dissolve** into other kinds of matter. If you put a teaspoon of sugar into a cup of water, it will look like it disappears. It dissolves into the water. If you taste the water, the sugar will still be there. The water will taste sweet. A solid such as sugar is **soluble** in a liquid like water. If you put an eyedropper of ink into a cup of water, it will mix completely with the water. All the water will be colored. No clear water will remain. This is also a demonstration of solubility. This experiment shows that two liquids can be soluble. Solids, liquids, and gases can all be soluble.

Conductivity is the ability of matter to allow heat or **electricity** to pass through it. You can see a demonstration of conductivity in your home every day. Most of the pots and pans in your kitchen have handles made of plastic or wood. Plastic and wood do not have good conductivity. Heat does not pass through them easily. It takes a long time for the handles to get hot. But metal has good conductivity. Most metals can **conduct** heat very easily. Handles made of these metals get hot very fast. To protect your hands from getting burned on a metal handle, you must use a thick cloth potholder. Cloth also has poor conductivity. Cloth will not get hot quickly.

In this reading you learned about the properties of matter. In the next reading, you will learn about atoms.

SELF-EVALUATION 3

VOCABULARY TICKETS

Read the vocabulary tickets with your teacher and the whole class. Are there still some words you do not understand? Write these words in a notebook. With a partner, write some example sentences using these new words. Talk about the meaning of these words with your classmates.

VOCABULARY CHECK

Here are some important words from this reading. Do you understand all of these words? Circle the words you do not understand. Then find the words in the reading. Talk about the meaning of these words with your classmates. If you know all the words, continue to the Question Review.

conduct	dissolve	sodium
conductivity	electricity	soluble
density	properties	solubility

QUESTION REVIEW

Go back to the questions on page 76. Look at your answers. Work with a partner. Look at your partner's answers too. Are they the same as your answers? Help each other write the correct answers.

PRE-READING 4

FOCUS QUESTION

Skim the reading on pages 79 and 80 to find the answer to the question below. Underline the answer in your book. Write the answer below.

■ *What are atoms?* _____

_____

DETAIL QUESTIONS

LEARNING STRATEGY
☆ **Reading selectively**

Read "Atoms" on pages 79 and 80. Find the details. Underline the answers in your book. Write the answers below. As you read, write down on your vocabulary tickets any words you do not understand or cannot pronounce.

1. What are three things that atoms are made of? _____

_____

2. What does orbit mean? _____

_____

3. What is the difference between a hypothesis and a theory?

_____

Atoms

In order to understand the makeup of matter, you need to know more about atoms. Atoms are the smallest particles of an element. Atoms can exist alone or in combination. They are too small to be seen without a special microscope. If you could see atoms, they would look like tiny planets with moons circling around them.

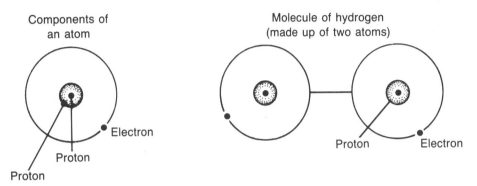

The diagram shows an oversimplified structure of an atom and a molecule of hydrogen with two atoms.

Atoms are made up of **neutrons**, **protons**, and **electrons**. Neutrons are particles of matter that contain no **electrical charge**. Protons are particles of matter that contain a positive (+) electrical charge. Protons and neutrons stick together in the center of the atom. The tiny moons that move around the **nucleus**, or center of the atom, are called electrons. They have very little mass compared to the heavier protons and neutrons. The electrons have a negative (−) electrical charge. They are attracted to the positive charge of the protons. The attraction is strong enough to pull the electrons toward the center. The high speed of the electrons keeps them in a kind of **orbit**, or curved path, around the protons and neutrons.

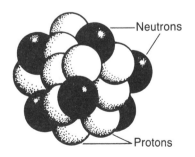

Protons and neutrons sticking together in the center of the atom

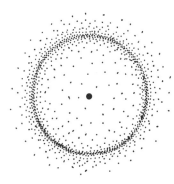

This diagram represents an orbit for the electron. You can see the electron cloud. The position of the electron may be anywhere in this cloud.

In order to answer questions, scientists form **theories**. A theory is an explanation for something that happens. For example, scientists formed a theory to explain the behavior of atoms. A theory is based on all known observations, facts, experimental results, and physical laws. In the activities and experiments in this chapter, you were working and learning like a scientist. Even when you did not know the answer, you wrote down your ideas. By doing these experiments and reading the chapter, you get more information. Your first idea about something is your **hypothesis**. If your first idea is still correct, you do not change your hypothesis, or idea. If your first idea is not correct, you change your hypothesis. This is how science makes progress. If after many years and hundreds of experiments and explanations, a hypothesis still seems to be the best or most accurate explanation, then it may become a theory.

SELF-EVALUATION 4

VOCABULARY TICKETS

Read the vocabulary tickets with your teacher and the whole class. Are there still some words you do not understand? Write these words in a notebook. With a partner, write some example sentences using these new words. Talk about the meaning of these words with your classmates.

VOCABULARY CHECK

Here are some important words from this reading. Do you understand all of these words? Circle the words you do not understand. Then find the words in the reading. Talk about the meaning of these words with your classmates. If you know all the words, continue to the Question Review.

electrical charge	neutrons	protons
electrons	nucleus	theories
hypothesis	orbit	

QUESTION REVIEW

Go back to the questions on page 78. Look at your answers. Work with a partner. Look at your partner's answers too. Are they the same as your answers? Help each other write the correct answers.

CHAPTER REVIEW

Now that you have completed your reading about matter, mass, and molecules, go back to pages 67 and 68. Look at your first ideas about matter, mass, and molecules. Have your ideas changed? What have you learned? Talk about your ideas with the teacher and the whole class.

EXTENSION ACTIVITIES

A. MAKING CHOICES

LEARNING STRATEGY

☆ **Synthesizing information**

Read the following statements. Decide which property of matter is being shown. Is it solubility? Is it density? Is it conductivity? Work with a partner. Help each other.

1. You put a teaspoon of instant coffee into a cup and add boiling water.
2. You put a piece of bread in the toaster and push the handle down to make some toast.
3. You put a piece of wood in water and it floats. You put a piece of metal in water and it sinks.
4. You lift the metal lid on a pot of rice and you burn your fingers.
5. You pour some thick chocolate syrup into a glass of milk and stir it to make a cup of chocolate milk.
6. You have a ¾-inch cork. You squeeze it into a ½-inch bottle.
7. You fill the washing machine with hot water and add soap powder.
8. You turn on the iron and iron your shirt.
9. You open a package of Jell-O®, pour the mix into the bowl and add boiling water.
10. You need a large plastic bag to hold one pound of mushrooms. One pound of carrots fits in a small bag.
11. You put your pie in a glass dish and put it into the oven to bake.
12. You turn on your hair dryer and dry your hair.
13. You drop two Alka-Seltzer® tablets into a glass of water.
14. Your sister sits down with a bottle of nail polish remover and takes the red polish off of her fingernails.

B. CROSSWORD PUZZLE

Use the clues to find the answers to the crossword puzzle that follows.

Crossword Clues

Across

3. A science activity or demonstration is called an

_____ .

4. An ice cube is an example of _____ matter.

10. Sugar or salt can _____ in water.

11. Matter comes in _____ basic states.

13. A _____ is made up of atoms.

14. A common water soluble liquid is _____.

15. Liquid, solid, and gas are the three basic _____ of matter.

17. It is in a gaseous state that molecules _____ fastest.

19. An _____ is the smallest possible part of an element.

21. _____ is the science that studies the form, elements, and makeup of matter.

23. There are two _____ atoms found in water.

24. Density, conductivity, and solubility are _____ of matter. They are ways of describing matter.

Down

1. Cooking pans made of _____ conduct heat well.

2. The states of matter are solid, gas, and _____.

3. Hydrogen, carbon, and oxygen are all examples of _____.

5. A water molecule has one atom of _____.

6. Water vapor is a _____.

7. There are over _____ elements to learn about.

8. Elements that allow heat or electricity pass through them have good _____.

9. _____ is an example of an element.

12. When we talk about how much matter can fit in a certain space, we are talking about _____.

16. _____ has one oxygen atom, and two hydrogen atoms.

18. Chemistry is a physical _____.

20. _____ is any material that takes up space.

22. The name of our world is the _____.

astronaut   A person who travels in outer space.

atom   The smallest particle of an element that can exist alone or in combinations.

carbon   A common element. The symbol for carbon is C.

chemistry   The science that studies the makeup and form of matter.

chlorine   A common element. The symbol for chlorine is Cl.

compound   A molecule made of different kinds of atoms.

conduct   To allow heat or electricity to pass through.

conductivity   The ability of matter to allow heat or electricity to pass through it.

density   The amount of matter that takes up a certain space.

dissolve   To mix completely into a liquid.

electrical charge   A force caused by the presence of electrons, protons, and other particles.

electricity   Energy from an electrical charge.

electrons   Parts of the atom; particles of matter that contain a negative electrical charge. Electrons move around the protons and neutrons.

element   An ingredient that can be combined with other ingredients. Elements make up the earth and everything on it.

gas   A state of matter; molecules are far apart and move very fast.

gaseous   The adjective for gas.

gravity   A force, or attraction, between two objects.

hydrogen   A common element. The symbol for hydrogen is H.

hypothesis   An educated guess; an idea for how and why something happens.

ingredients   Separate things you need to make something.

liquid   A state of matter; the molecules in a liquid are farther apart and move faster than the molecules in a solid.

mass   The amount of matter in an object.

matter   Anything that takes up space and has mass.

molecule   The smallest part of certain substances. A molecule is made up of one or more atoms.

naked eye   To see without the help of a machine to make it larger.

neutrons   Parts of the atom; particles of matter that contain no electrical charge.

nucleus   The center of the atom; contains the protons and neutrons. Electrons orbit the nucleus.

orbit   A circular or elliptical path.

oxygen   A common element. The symbol for oxygen is O.

particle   A small amount of matter.

physics   The science that studies matter, energy, motion, and force.

properties   Features, or characteristics, of things. You describe something by talking about its properties such as color, weight, odor, and taste.

protons   Parts of the atom; particles of matter that contain a positive electrical charge.

pure element   A molecule made of only one kind of atom.

sodium   A common element.

solid   A state of matter; molecules are close together and move slowly.

solubility   The ability of matter to dissolve into other kinds of matter.

soluble   The adjective form of solubility.

state   The form of matter; solid, liquid, or gas.

symbol   One or two letters that make up the abbreviation for an element.

theories   The best and most accurate explanations for how and why things happen.

water vapor   The gaseous state of water.

weight   The heaviness of something, caused by the pull of gravity.

CHAPTER

5 PHYSICS

MOTION AND NEWTON'S LAWS OF MOTION

Physics is the science that explains how the world around us is put together and why things happen the way they do. For example, physics tells us why the sky is blue and how the sun gives off light and heat. Newton's laws of motion help us to understand why things move the way they do. In this chapter, you will study about motion and Newton's laws of motion.

WHAT DO YOU ALREADY KNOW ABOUT MOTION?

LEARNING STRATEGIES
☆ Using prior knowledge
☆ Working cooperatively

Read these sentences. Draw a circle around the words you do not understand. Underline the words you cannot pronounce.

Speed can be measured in miles per hour.

Motion is the change in position of an object.

Isaac Newton studied motion.

An object cannot accelerate by itself.

An astronaut in outer space may be weightless.

Sit down with a partner. Look at your book and your partner's book. Help each other understand the words that are circled. Help each other pronounce the words that are underlined.

THINK ABOUT THESE IDEAS

LEARNING STRATEGIES
☆ Sequencing
☆ Inferencing
☆ Self-evaluation

Sit down in groups of three or four. Work together to answer these questions. If you are not sure about your answers, guess!

1. How fast does it go? In your group, decide how to put the things below in the correct order from the fastest to the slowest. Try to agree with each other. Write number 1 next to the one that is the fastest and number 10 next to the one that is the slowest.

_____ motorcycle

_____ train

_____ skateboard

_____ race car

_____ tractor

_____ bicycle

_____ rollerskates

_____ row boat

_____ jet plane

_____ ship

When you finish numbering these forms of transportation, write down the speed for each one, for example, 20 miles per hour (mph).

2. If you stand on a chair or desk and drop a nail and a feather at the same time, the nail will hit the ground before the feather. If you drop two balls from the same height, one about twice as large and heavy as the other one, they will hit the ground at the same time. In your groups, discuss why this happens. Write down the ideas from your group in your notebook.

When your group finishes talking about these ideas, share your ideas with the whole class. Are your ideas different? Are they similar? After you read this chapter, look at these ideas and your answers again. Do not worry if your answers are right or wrong.

GROUP OBSERVATIONS

LEARNING STRATEGIES
☆ Inferencing
☆ Taking notes
☆ Self-evaluation

Materials

a large ball	a piece of visible tape
balloons	a pail of water

Sit down in groups of three or four. Read the questions below and talk about what you see, feel, or hear. Remember, this is not a test.

1. Pushing: Two students will need to volunteer for this activity. You will need a large ball (a basketball, volleyball, etc.). One student will roll the ball gently from the front of the class to the back of the class. About halfway, another student should give the ball a gentle push in the same direction it is moving. What happened to the ball? Why did this happen? Discuss this in your group. Did the ball slow down or speed up? Write your own ideas in your notebook. What would eventually happen to the ball if no one touched it after the first push? Why would this happen?

2. Balloons: Your teacher or classmate will blow up a balloon and hold the end of the balloon closed, and then let go of the balloon. Watch carefully. Then, try to explain what happened. In your group, discuss why you think this happened. Write your ideas in your notebook.

3. Quick stop: Your teacher will put a large piece of tape on the floor of the classroom. One student will run toward the tape and stop directly behind the tape. Two students will try to stop as closely as they can to the tape. Watch what happens when the students try to stop. In your group, discuss why this happens. Write your ideas in your notebook.

4. Pail of water: Your teacher will put a little water in the bottom of a pail, then swing the pail with the water in it overhead several times. The water will stay in the pail even when it is upside down. Why does this happen? In your group, discuss why this happens. Write your ideas in your notebook.

Share your ideas with the whole class. After you finish reading this chapter, come back to these questions and observations and read them again. Are your answers the same?

FOCUS QUESTION

Skim the reading on pages 88, 89, 90, and 91 to find the answer to the question below. Underline the answer in your book. Write the answer below.

■ *What are three things we need to understand when we discuss*

motion? _____

_____

DETAIL QUESTIONS

Read "Speed, Velocity and Acceleration" on pages 88, 89, 90, and 91. Find the details. Underline the answers in your book. Write the answers below. As you read, write down on your vocabulary tickets any words you do not understand or cannot pronounce.

LEARNING STRATEGY
☆ **Reading selectively**

1. What is speed? _____

_____

2. What is the formula for speed? _____

_____

3. What is velocity? _____

_____

4. What does constant speed and constant velocity mean? _____

_____

5. What does changing velocity mean for the motion of an object?

_____

_____

6. What is acceleration? _____

_____

READING 1 ★

Speed, Velocity, and Acceleration

Riding a bicycle is fun, and it is good exercise. When you ride a bicycle, roller skate, or drive a car, you can learn some interesting facts about the study of **motion**. Motion is the change in position of an object. When we discuss motion, we must understand three words: **speed**, **velocity**, and **acceleration**.

Speed is the **rate** at which a distance is covered, or the distance an object moves in a certain amount of time. For example, imagine that you wanted to drive to another city that is 110 miles away. It takes you two hours to drive the distance. The **formula** for speed is the distance traveled divided by the time it takes to get there. Study the example below.

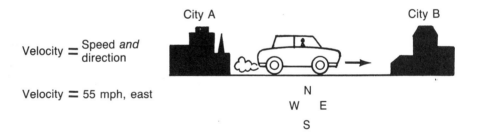

$$\text{Speed} = \frac{\text{Distance}}{\text{Time}}$$

$$\text{Speed} = \frac{110 \text{ Miles}}{2 \text{ hours}} = 55 \text{ Mph}$$

Time = 1 hour

If you divide 110 by 2, you get 55. In the example, we talk about speed in miles per hour (mph). We can talk about speed in other units of distance and time, for example, kilometers and seconds.

Velocity is the speed and direction of motion. In everyday speech, speed and velocity are often used to mean the same thing. When we talk about motion, we use them to mean different things. If you say that your car is going 55 mph, that is speed. If you say that your car is going 55 mph north, that is velocity. If you hear a weather reporter say that the wind is blowing 25 mph northeast, that is the velocity of the wind.

Velocity = Speed *and* direction

Velocity = 55 mph, east

Constant speed and constant velocity mean that an object is moving at the same speed in the same direction. In other words, the object is moving at the same speed in a straight line.

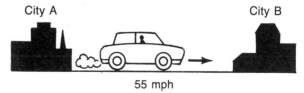

55 mph

No change in speed = constant speed
No change in direction = constant velocity

Constant speed and changing velocity mean that an object is moving at the same speed along a curved path. Direction on a curved path is changing every **instant**. The velocity is changing because the direction is changing.

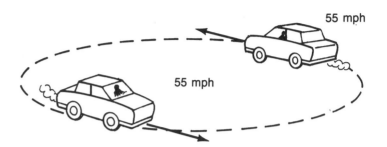

Change in direction but *not* speed = constant speed, changing velocity

It is also possible to have changing speed and changing velocity.

Change in speed *and* change in direction

A third important property of motion is acceleration. The rate of change in velocity is acceleration. We have learned that we can change the state of motion by changing the speed, by changing the direction, or by changing both the speed and direction. The formula for acceleration is the change of velocity divided by the time.

$$\text{acceleration} = \frac{\text{change of velocity}}{\text{time}}$$

For example, imagine you are driving a car. You increase your velocity 10 mph in one minute, from 35 mph to 45 mph. In the next minute, you increase your velocity 10 mph, from 45 mph to 55 mph. This change in velocity is called acceleration. In this example, acceleration is the change each minute in velocity.

$$\text{acceleration} = \frac{10 \text{ mph}}{1 \text{ minute}}$$

If you divide 10 (mph) by 1 (minute), you will get 10. The acceleration is 10 miles every minute.

The man on the motorcycle is experiencing acceleration.

The word acceleration means decreases as well as increases in velocity. The brakes of a car produce **negative acceleration**. They can slow you down.

Acceleration occurs when you step on the gas and when you step on the brake.

Acceleration occurs when there is a change in a state of motion. Velocity is the rate at which the position changes. Acceleration is the rate at which velocity changes.

In this reading you learned three important concepts about motion. In the next reading, you will learn about Newton's first law of motion.

SELF-EVALUATION 1

VOCABULARY TICKETS

Read the vocabulary tickets with your teacher and the whole class. Are there still some words you do not understand? Write these words in a notebook. With a partner, write some example sentences using these new words. Talk about the meaning of these words with your classmates.

VOCABULARY CHECK

Here are some important words from this reading. Do you understand all of these words? Circle the words you do not understand. Then find the words in the reading. Talk about the meaning of these words with your classmates. If you know all the words, continue to the the Question Review.

acceleration	instant	rate
constant	motion	speed
formula	negative acceleration	velocity

QUESTION REVIEW

Go back to the questions on page 88. Look at your answers. Work with a partner. Look at your partner's answers too. Are they the same as your answers? Help each other write the correct answers.

FOCUS QUESTION

Skim the reading on pages 92, 93, and 94 to find the answer to the question below. Underline the answer in your book. Write the answer below.

■ *What is the first law of motion?* _____

_____

DETAIL QUESTIONS

LEARNING STRATEGY
☆ **Reading selectively**

Read "Newton's First Law of Motion" on pages 92, 93, and 94. Find the details. Underline the answers in your book. Write the answers below. As you read, write down on your vocabulary tickets any words you do not understand or cannot pronounce.

1. Who developed the laws of motion? When? _____

_____

2. What is a force? _____

_____

3. What happens to an object if you apply a force? _____

_____

4. What is inertia? _____

_____

READING 2 ★

Newton's First Law of Motion

Understanding motion and why things move the way they do is a problem scientists have studied for many years. The study of motion began with Aristotle in the fourth century B.C. and continued for almost 2,000 years. Then, in the 1600s Isaac Newton developed the famous laws of motion. Newton's laws explain why things move the way they do.

Before you read on, remember that there are often many different laws working together at the same time. For example, the laws of motion and the law of **gravity** work together at the same time. Gravity pulls things to the earth. Sometimes this makes it seem like the laws are not working. It makes it difficult to understand the laws. While reading

Newton's laws, remember that they apply to objects in a **vacuum**. There is no air in a vacuum. There is no air in outer space. There is nothing for an object to **resist**. There is nothing to stop the object or to slow it down.

Law 1: Every object at **rest** stays at rest and every object in motion stays in motion in a straight line unless a **force** is applied to it.

In other words, an object continues doing what it is doing unless a force is applied to it. A force is a push or a pull.

The boat will remain at rest unless the force of the wind moves it.

If an object is at rest, or not moving, it stays at rest. If an object is moving, it continues to move. It will move in a straight line without turning or changing speeds if it is in a vacuum. In a normal environment, a moving object may slow down because of the **friction** or **resistance**, that is, something in the object's way that stops it or slows it down. In a vacuum, or a **frictionless environment** or place, it would keep on moving. The important thing to remember is that an object cannot accelerate by itself. It needs a force.

The force of the hand accelerates the brick.

The force of the man accelerates the skating elephant.

Inertia is another concept you need to understand when learning about Newton's first law of motion. Inertia is the resistance an object has to motion or the ability an object has to continue in its state of motion. Every object has inertia. How much inertia an object has depends on the mass of the object. The more mass an object has, the more inertia it will have. Box A in the picture has less inertia than Box B. Box A will be easier to move than Box B.

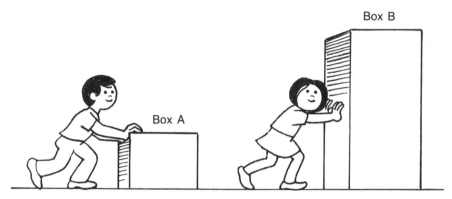

Which box has more inertia, A or B? Both boxes contain sand.

Remember that mass and weight are not the same thing. The amount of matter an object has is mass. Weight is caused by the pull of gravity on an object. A **weightless** object with mass is still difficult to move.

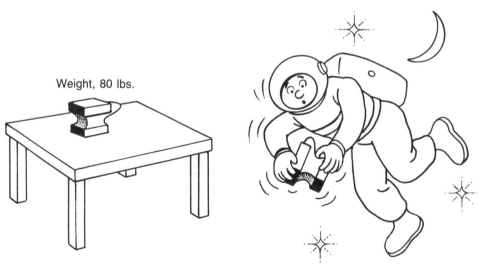

An anvil in outer space may be weightless, but it is not massless. The astronaut in outer space will find it just as difficult to shake the weightless anvil as an anvil with weight.

In this reading you learned about Newton's first law of motion. In the next reading, you will continue reading about motion. You will read about Newton's second law of motion.

VOCABULARY TICKETS

Read the vocabulary tickets with your teacher and the whole class. Are there still some words you do not understand? Write these words in a notebook. With a partner, write some example sentences using these new words. Talk about the meaning of these words with your classmates.

VOCABULARY CHECK

Here are some important words from this reading. Do you understand all of these words? Circle the words you do not understand. Then find the words in the reading. Talk about the meaning of these words with your classmates. If you know all the words, continue to the Question Review.

force	resist
friction	resistance
frictionless environment	rest
gravity	vacuum
inertia	weightless

QUESTION REVIEW

Go back to the questions on page 92. Look at your answers. Work with a partner. Look at your partner's answers too. Are they the same as your answers? Help each other write the correct answers.

PRE-READING 3

FOCUS QUESTION

Skim the reading on pages 96, 97, 98, and 99 to find the answer to the question below. Underline the answer in the reading. Write the answer below.

■ *What is Newton's second law of motion?* _____

_____

DETAIL QUESTIONS

Read "Newton's Second Law of Motion" on pages 96, 97, 98, and 99. Find the details. Underline the answers in your book. Write the answers below. As you read, write down on your vocabulary tickets any words you do not understand or cannot pronounce.

┌─────────────────────┐
│ **LEARNING STRATEGY** │
│ ☆ **Reading selectively** │
└─────────────────────┘

1. In which direction will an object accelerate? _____

_____

2. What happens when you use the same force with two bricks

instead of one brick? _____

_____

3. What happens when you use the same force with three bricks instead of one brick? _____

_____

4. What happens when you double the force with one brick?

_____

_____

5. What happens when you double the force and double the number of bricks? _____

_____

6. Why do falling balls of different weights and masses hit the ground at the same time? _____

_____

7. Why do a feather and a rock hit the ground at different times?

_____

_____

READING 3 ★

Newton's Second Law of Motion

The relationship of acceleration to force and inertia is explained in Newton's second law.

Law 2: The acceleration of an object depends on the mass of the object and the size and direction of the force applied to it.

An object accelerates in the direction of the force acting on it.

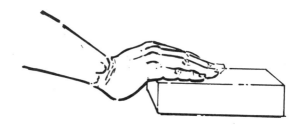

The force of a hand accelerates the brick. The brick is moving in the direction of the force. For example, in the activity you did with your classmates before you started your reading in this chapter, you demonstrated Newton's second law of motion. One classmate gently pushed a ball in a straight line. Midway, another classmate pushed the ball again. The force, or push, was in the direction the ball was moving. There was an increase in speed or velocity.

If you use the same force of one hand with two bricks instead of one brick, there will be more inertia. The bricks will accelerate only half as much.

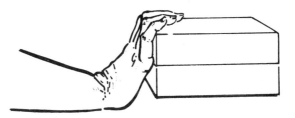

If you use the same force of one hand with three bricks, the bricks will accelerate only one-third as much.

If you have two hands or twice as much force on one brick, it will produce twice as much acceleration.

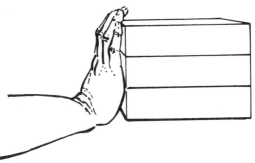

Two bricks will have twice the mass of one brick. If you use twice the force on twice the mass, the acceleration will be the same as for one hand on one brick.

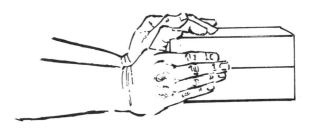

Galileo Galilei, who lived between 1564 and 1652, also studied motion. In his famous demonstration at the Leaning Tower of Pisa, Galileo showed us an important principle. He dropped two objects of different weights and masses from the top of the tower. Galileo knew that objects released at the same time, would hit the ground at the same time. Weight and mass differences would not matter. Galileo did not understand why this was true. Newton understood this concept and began to **formulate** a theory to explain it. This is Newton's theory of **gravitational force**. This theory says that a falling object is pulled toward earth by a constant force called a gravitational force. Gravity keeps things on the earth.

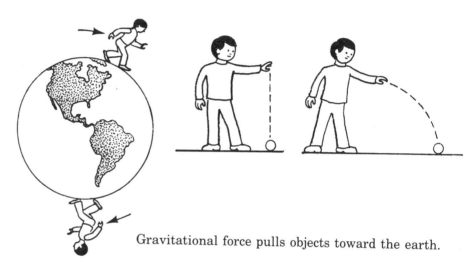

Gravitational force pulls objects toward the earth.

If you drop two balls of different weights and masses from the top of a building, the two balls will hit the ground at the same time. Why is this true? The larger ball will have more gravitational pull toward the earth. But it will also have more inertia to resist the force. Inertia is the reason that two objects with different weights and masses, such as the balls, hit the ground at the same time.

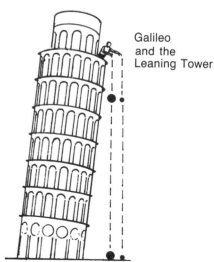

Galileo and the Leaning Tower

The larger object hits the ground at the same time as the smaller object because of the relationship between inertia and gravitational force. An object with twice as much mass has twice as much gravitational pull as the smaller object. It also has twice as much inertia to slow it down. This means that the two objects will hit the ground at the same time. Gravity remains constant.

If you take a stone and a feather and drop them at the same time from a tall building, they will not hit the ground at the same time. Why is this true? The answer is **air resistance**. The feather reacts differently to the air. If you put the stone and the feather in a vacuum, they would fall at the same speed. There would be no air resistance. There is no air in a vacuum.

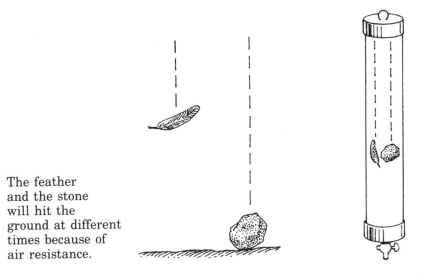

The feather and the stone will hit the ground at different times because of air resistance.

In the next reading you will learn about Newton's third law of motion.

SELF-EVALUATION 3

VOCABULARY TICKETS

Read the vocabulary tickets with your teacher and the whole class. Are there still some words you do not understand? Write these words in a notebook. With a partner, write some example sentences using these new words. Talk about the meaning of these words with your classmates.

VOCABULARY CHECK

Here are some important words from this reading. Do you understand all of these words? Circle the words you do not understand. Then find the words in the reading. Talk about the meaning of these words with your classmates. If you know all the words, continue to the Question Review.

air resistance   gravitational force
formulate

QUESTION REVIEW

Go back to the questions on pages 95 and 96. Look at your answers. Work with a partner. Look at your partner's answers too. Are they the same as your answers? Help each other write the correct answers.

FOCUS QUESTION

Skim the reading on pages 101 and 102 to find the answer to the question below. Underline the answer in your book. Write the answer below.

■ *What is Newton's third law of motion?* _____

_____

DETAIL QUESTIONS

LEARNING STRATEGY
☆ **Reading selectively**

Read "Newton's Third Law of Motion" on pages 101 and 102. Find the details. Underline the answers in your book. Write the answers below. As you read, write down on your vocabulary tickets any words you do not understand or cannot pronounce.

1. A rolling tire pushing on the road is an action; what is the reaction? _____

_____

2. A rocket pushing on the gas is an action; what is the reaction?

_____

_____

3. A man pulling on a spring is the action; what is the reaction?

_____

_____

4. When Galileo dropped the objects from the Leaning Tower of Pisa, what was the action and the reaction? _____

_____

5. Can you touch someone without being touched? Why? _____

_____

6. Think of two examples of Newton's third law of motion at work in your daily life. _____

_____

Newton's Third Law of Motion

Newton's third law of motion is usually stated in the following way:

Law 3: For every **action** there is an equal and opposite **reaction**.

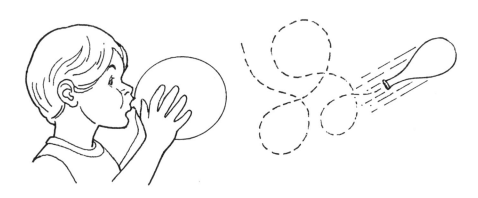

In the activity you did with your classmates before you began reading this chapter, you demonstrated Newton's third law of motion. Blowing up the balloon was the action. Air coming out of the balloon was the reaction.

Forces always come in pairs. There is never a single force in any situation. It does not matter which force is called an action and which is called a reaction. One does not exist without the other. When a car moves along the road, the action is the tire pushing on the road. The reaction is the road pushing on the tire.

When a rocket takes off, the action is the rocket pushing on the gas. The reaction is the gas pushing on the rocket.

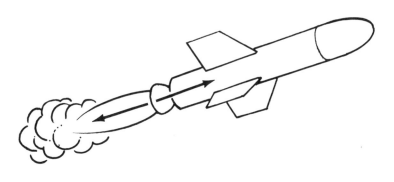

When a man pulls on a **spring**, the action is the man pulling on the spring. The reaction is the spring pulling on the man.

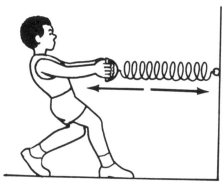

You can see Newton's third law of motion at work everywhere. All forces, whether they are large or small, always occur in pairs. Forces are **interactions** between different things. For example, a fish swimming in the river is demonstrating this law. The fish pushes the water backward with its fins, the water pushes the fish forward. The wind pushes against the branches in the trees. The trees push against the wind. It is impossible to touch someone or something without being touched back. Think of more examples from everyday life where Newton's third law of motion is at work.

SELF-EVALUATION 4

VOCABULARY TICKETS

Read the vocabulary tickets with your teacher and the whole class. Are there still some words you do not understand? Write these words in a notebook. With a partner, write some example sentences using these new words. Talk about the meaning of these words with your classmates.

VOCABULARY CHECK

Here are some important words from this reading. Do you understand all of these words? Circle the words you do not understand. Then find the words in the reading. Talk about the meaning of these words with your classmates. If you know all the words, continue to the Question Review.

action   reaction

interactions   spring

QUESTION REVIEW

Go back to the questions on page 100. Look at your answers. Work with a partner. Look at your partner's answers too. Are they the same as your answers? Help each other write the correct answers.

CHAPTER REVIEW

Now that you have completed your reading about the laws of motion, go back to pages 86 and 87. Look at your first ideas about motion. Have your ideas changed? What have you learned? Talk about your ideas with the teacher and the whole class.

A. MAKING CHOICES

Sit down in groups of three or four. With your group members, try to match the words in column A to the ideas in Column B.

Column A	Column B
_____ 1. inertia	a. a Greek philosopher and scientist who first studied motion
_____ 2. velocity	b. interactions
_____ 3. speed	c. a stone and a feather fall together
_____ 4. force	d. 50 mph
_____ 5. acceleration	e. stepping on the gas pedal
_____ 6. at rest	f. the Leaning Tower of Pisa
_____ 7. Isaac Newton	g. resistance to change
_____ 8. Aristotle	h. 50 mph north
_____ 9. Galileo	i. the wind blowing a sail
_____ 10. reaction	j. made a formula for
_____ 11. formulated	k. a car parked in a parking lot
_____ 12. weightless	l. the spring pulling against the man
_____ 13. vacuum	m. laws of motion
_____ 14. forces	n. an astronaut in space

B. DISCUSSION QUESTIONS

Sit down with three or four classmates in a group. Read and discuss the following questions together. Write your answers in your notebook. When your teacher calls time, share your answers with the entire class.

LEARNING STRATEGIES

☆ **Using prior knowledge**

☆ **Working cooperatively**

---

1. You are playing kickball. You kick the ball against the wall. The ball hits the wall and bounces back to you. Which of Newton's laws of motion does this demonstrate? Explain your answer.
2. Why is it possible to jump higher if you are on the moon rather than on Earth?
3. You are playing baseball. You hit the ball with the bat. The ball goes forward, straight into the field. You score a home run. Which of Newton's laws of motion does this demonstrate?
4. Use Newton's third law of motion to explain why you cannot decrease your weight when standing on a scale by pulling up on the laces of your shoes.

5. Which ball will hit the ground faster if a basketball and a tennis ball are dropped at the same time from the top of a 20-story building? Why?

C. NEW IDEAS ABOUT MOTION

Work in groups. Try not to use your books! Use the words below to complete the sentences that follow.

Newton	massless	action
Galileo	at rest	velocity
forces	direction	laws

1. Interactions between objects are called _____.

2. The Leaning Tower of Pisa is famous because _____ did his famous demonstration there.

3. An astronaut in outer space may be weightless but not

_____.

4. For every _____ there is an equal and opposite

reaction.

5. Velocity is speed and the _____ of the speed.

6. When an object is not moving, we say it is _____

_____. (two words)

7. Speed and the direction of speed is called _____.

8. Scientific discoveries made by Isaac Newton are called the

_____ of motion.

9. A mathematician and physicist named _____

discovered many important ideas about motion.

Aristotle	constant	motion
gravity	inertia	speed
vacuum	equal	acceleration

10. A Greek philosopher and scientist who first studied motion was

_____.

11. The earth is in a _____ state of motion.

12. Another word for movement is _____.

13. To speed up or slow down is called _____.

14. An object is pulled toward the earth by _____.

15. The three important properties of motion are _____, velocity, and acceleration.

16. An elephant will have more _____, or resistance to motion than a small dog.

17. For every action, there is an _____ and opposite reaction.

18. A space where there is no air is called a _____.

GLOSSARY

acceleration The rate of change in velocity; change in velocity divided by the time.

action Movement; the way an object moves or works.

air resistance The force of air pulling or pushing against an object.

constant Not changing.

force A push or pull.

formula A method, or way of doing something or saying something.

formulate Put into a formula; to find a formula for.

friction Resistance to movement or motion.

frictionless environment A place with no friction or resistance.

gravitational force The force that attracts objects to the earth.

gravity A pull or force toward the center of the earth.

inertia The resistance an object has to motion.

instant A moment; a very short time.

interactions Actions on or with something else.

motion The change in position of an object.

negative acceleration Slow down; a decrease in velocity.

rate An amount of something considered in relationship to a unit of something else.

reaction A response to an action or force.

resist To fight against the action or effect of something.

resistance The act of resisting; the noun form of resist.

rest No movement.

speed The rate at which a distance is covered.

spring A wire that keeps its shape after it is bent and pulled.

vacuum An empty space with no air.

velocity The speed and direction of motion; for example, 50 mph north.

weightless Without weight.

6 ASTRONOMY
THE SOLAR SYSTEM

INTRODUCTION

In previous chapters you learned about the Earth. You learned about the land formations, weather, and oceans of Earth. You also learned what things are made of and how and why objects move. In this chapter you will learn about other planets besides Earth. You will also learn about the stars and the sun. The study of other planets and the stars is called **astronomy**.

CRITICAL THINKING ACTIVITIES

WHAT DO YOU ALREADY KNOW ABOUT THE SOLAR SYSTEM?

Read these sentences. Draw a circle around the words you do not understand. Underline the words you cannot pronounce.

The sun is yellow-orange.
The sun gives us heat and light.
Jupiter is the name of a planet.
The Earth has one satellite called the moon.
Mercury is the planet closest to the sun.
Stars are very far away from the Earth.

Sit down with a partner. Look at your book and your partner's book. Help each other understand the words that are circled. Help each other pronounce the words that are underlined.

LEARNING STRATEGIES

☆ Using prior knowledge
☆ Working cooperatively

THINK ABOUT THESE IDEAS

Work in groups of three or four. Work together to answer these questions. Record your group's answers in your notebook. If you are not sure about your answers, guess!

1. Name five different ways people use the sun in everyday life.
2. Think of three differences between a star and a planet.
3. Look at the pictures and then answer the questions below. You can have more than one answer for each question.

   a. Which of these bodies revolves around Earth?
   b. Which are planets?

LEARNING STRATEGIES

☆ Working cooperatively
☆ Taking notes
☆ Self-evaluation

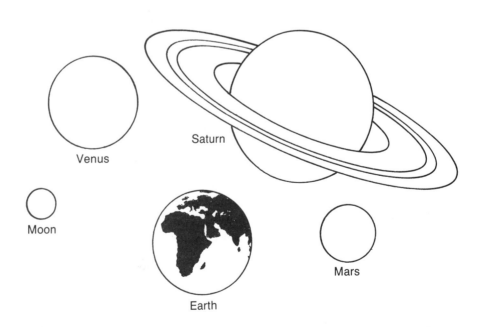

Venus

Saturn

Moon

Earth

Mars

c. Which ones revolve in orbits around the sun?
d. Which is nearest to Earth?
e. Which has plants and animals?
f. Which are larger than Earth?

When your group finishes talking about these ideas, share your ideas with the whole class. Are your ideas different? Are they similar? After you read this chapter, look at these ideas and your answers again. Do not worry if your answers are right or wrong.

GROUP OBSERVATIONS

Work in groups of three or four.

LEARNING STRATEGIES
☆ Imagery
☆ Self-evaluation

1. Work together with your group. Decide how you will demonstrate the following things.

a. How the Earth rotates
b. How the Earth revolves around the sun
c. How the Earth revolves and rotates at the same time
d. How the moon revolves around the Earth

Materials

paper	a ruler	string	pencils	pens

2. Work with your group to make a chart showing the size of the Earth, Venus, and the moon. Use the information below to help you. Begin by making the Earth, moon, and Venus in the correct sizes. Put them around the room by using the following information.

a. The **diameter** of Earth is four times that of the moon.
b. Venus and Earth are almost the same size.
c. Ten trips around the Earth is equal to a one-way trip to the moon.
d. One hundred trips to the moon from Earth is equal to a one-way trip to Venus.

Share your answers with the whole class. After you finish reading this chapter, come back to these questions and observations and read them again. Are your answers the same?

PRE-READING 1

FOCUS QUESTION

Skim the reading on pages 109, 110, and 111 to find the answer to the question below. Underline the answer in your book. Write the answer below.

■ *What is a solar system?* _____

_____

DETAIL QUESTIONS

Read "The Sun and the Solar System" on pages 109, 110, and 111. Find the details. Underline the answers in your book. Write the answers below. As you read, write down on your vocabulary tickets any words you do not understand or cannot pronounce.

LEARNING STRATEGY
☆ **Reading selectively**

1. What is the nearest star to Earth? _____

_____

2. What are solar winds? _____

_____

3. What is atmosphere? _____

_____

4. How far is the sun from Earth? _____

_____

5. What are stars? _____

_____

6. What is a satellite? _____

_____

7. Name the principal planets in our solar system. _____

_____

8. What type of an orbit do planets move in? _____

_____

READING 1 ★

The Sun and the Solar System

The **stars** we see in the sky at night are balls of gas that send out heat and light. Most stars are very far away. We see only a small **twinkle** of off-and-on light and feel no heat from them. The nearest star to the Earth is the sun. We see its light and feel its heat. Stars are many different sizes. Some are much larger than our sun and some are smaller.

The surface of our sun is very hot. It is about 10,000° Fahrenheit. The surface of the sun has many storms. During these storms gases escape into outer space. The movement of the gases is called **solar wind**. The center of the sun is even hotter than the surface. It is about 27,000° Fahrenheit. Very little of the heat and light given off by the sun ever reaches the Earth. Most of the heat and light is lost in space during the 8 minutes and 20 seconds it takes for the light to travel. The heat and light that finally reach the Earth are trapped by the Earth's **atmosphere**. Atmosphere is a mixture of gases that surrounds a planet. The heat from the sun warms the Earth's surface. The atmosphere will not let the heat escape.

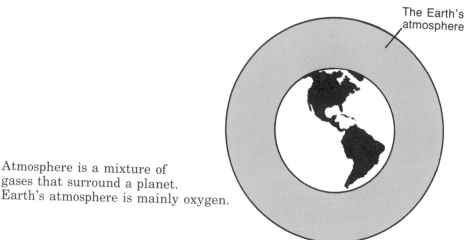

The Earth's atmosphere

Atmosphere is a mixture of gases that surround a planet. Earth's atmosphere is mainly oxygen.

Earth is 93 million miles, or 150 million kilometers, from the sun. If Earth were much closer to the sun, the temperature on Earth would be too high. It would be impossible for plants and animals to live. If Earth were much farther away from the sun, it would be too cold for animals and plants to live. It is hard to imagine how far away the sun is from the Earth. If you wanted to drive to the sun, it would take you about 200 years.

The sun is the center of our **solar system** and the nearest star. A solar system is a group of planets and their **satellites** that **orbit**, or **revolve**, around a star. A satellite is a **celestial body** orbiting a planet. For example, the moon is a satellite of Earth. Earth has only one satellite. Some planets have more than one satellite.

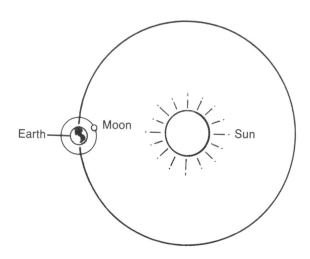

Earth — Moon — Sun

Besides the planet Earth there are eight other **principal planets** in our solar system. These planets move in **elliptical** orbits around the sun. An elliptical orbit is in the shape of an oval, or a flattened circle.

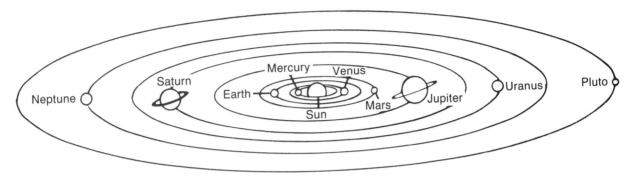

Planets move in elliptical orbits around the sun.

Six of the nine planets were known to the early scientists who first studied the stars. These planets are Mercury, Venus, Earth, Mars, Jupiter, and Saturn. These planets are the closest to the Earth and to the sun. The other three planets were discovered in modern times. They are Uranus, Neptune, and Pluto. The planets vary in size. If you chose a pea to represent Mercury, the planet closest to the sun, you could use a cherry tomato to represent Earth. A very large pumpkin would represent Jupiter, the largest planet.

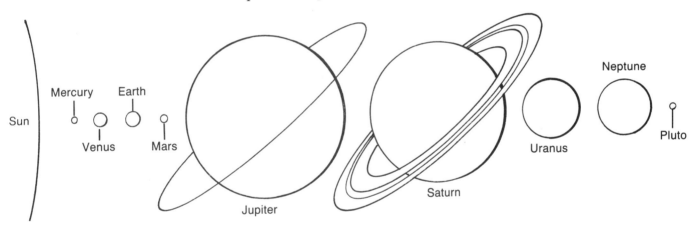

In this reading you learned about the solar system. In the next readings you will learn more about the nine principal planets that make up our solar system.

SELF-EVALUATION 1

VOCABULARY TICKETS

Read the vocabulary tickets with your teacher and the whole class. Are there still some words you do not understand? Write these words in a notebook. With a partner, write some example sentences using these new words. Talk about the meaning of these words with your classmates.

VOCABULARY CHECK

Here are some important words from this reading. Do you understand all of these words? Circle the words you do not understand. Then find the words in the reading. Talk about the meaning of these words with your classmates. If you know all the words, continue to the Question Review.

atmosphere	principal planets	solar wind
celestial body	revolve	stars
elliptical	satellites	twinkle
orbit	solar system	

QUESTION REVIEW

Go back to the questions on pages 108 and 109. Look at your answers. Work with a partner. Look at your partner's answers too. Are they the same as your answers? Help each other write the correct answers.

PRE-READING 2

FOCUS QUESTION

Skim the reading on pages 113 and 114 to find the answer to the question below. Underline the answer in your book. Write the answer below.

■ *What three planets are closest to Earth?* _____

_____

DETAIL QUESTIONS

Read "The Planets Closest to the Earth" on pages 113 and 114. Find the details. Underline the answers in your book. Write the answers below.
As you read, write down on your vocabulary tickets any words you do not understand or cannot pronounce.

> **LEARNING STRATEGY**
>
> ☆ **Reading selectively**

1. Which planet is closest to the sun? _____

_____

2. How long does it take Mercury to go around the sun? _____

_____

3. What are the daytime and nighttime temperatures on the surface

of Mercury? _____

_____

4. Describe the surface of Mercury. _____

_____

5. How far away from the sun is Venus? _____

_____

6. Name three differences between the Earth and Venus.

_____

_____

7. What is another name for Mars? _____

_____

READING 2 ★

The Planets Closest to the Earth

In this reading you will learn about the three planets in our solar system that are closest to Earth. Look at the diagram of our solar system. What three planets are closest to Earth?

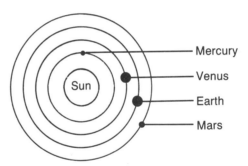

The planet closest to the sun is Mercury. It is only 36 million miles from the sun. It is also a small planet, about one-half the size of Earth. It has a **diameter** of 3,000 miles. Mercury revolves around the sun every 88 days.

Because Mercury is small, the surface gravity is only two-fifths the gravity of Earth. You could jump like a grasshopper on Mercury. But, you would not want to touch the surface of Mercury. In the daytime, Mercury's surface is more than 800° Fahrenheit. At night, the temperature drops to −275° Fahrenheit. The surface of Mercury is filled with **craters**, or large holes, and covered by ridges and cliffs. It looks like the surface of the moon.

Venus is closer to the sun than Earth is. Venus is the brightest, or most **brilliant** object in the sky. Sometimes Venus is called the morning star or evening star because it is so bright. Of course, Venus is not a star. It is one of the major planets in our solar system. Only the sun and the moon are brighter than Venus. Venus is 67,270,000 miles from the sun and 25 million miles from Earth. It revolves around the sun every 225 days. Venus is about the same size as Earth. It has a diameter of 7,700 miles.

Venus may appear similar to Earth in size, but it is very different in other ways. First, Venus **rotates**, or spins, **clockwise**, or in the same direction as the hands on a clock. Except for Venus, all the other planets in our solar system rotate **counterclockwise**.

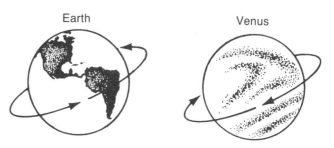

Earth   Venus

A second difference is that the rotation of Venus is very slow. It takes Venus 243 days to make a complete rotation. This is longer than it takes Venus to go around the sun. This is not true for other planets in our solar system. The third important difference between Venus and Earth is the atmosphere. The atmosphere on Venus could not support life as we know it. It is dense and cloudy with almost 90 percent carbon dioxide and no oxygen.

Mars is called the red planet because it has a reddish color. It is the planet nearest to Earth. Mars is smaller than Earth. It has a diameter of 4,200 miles. It rotates once every 24 hours and 37 minutes. It takes 687 days to revolve around the sun. Mars has two tiny satellites.

The atmosphere on Mars is made up of carbon dioxide. There is very little water, oxygen, or nitrogen that is so important to life on Earth. Mars has no **ozone layer**, or oxygen, in its atmosphere to keep out the harmful rays of the sun. The atmosphere on Mars would not be suitable for life as we know it. The temperature on the surface ranges from 86° Fahrenheit in the day to −103° Fahrenheit at night. The surface of the planet is covered with rocks, huge boulders, mountains, craters, and deep canyons.

In this reading you learned some important facts about Venus, Mercury, and Mars, the three planets closest to Earth. In the next reading, you will learn about the planets in our solar system that are farthest from our sun and from Earth.

SELF-EVALUATION 2

VOCABULARY TICKETS

Read the vocabulary tickets with your teacher and the whole class. Are there still some words you do not understand? Write these words in a notebook. With a partner, write some example sentences using these new words. Talk about the meaning of these words with your classmates.

VOCABULARY CHECK

Here are some important words from this reading. Do you understand all of these words? Circle the words you do not understand. Then find the words in the reading. Talk about the meaning of these words with your classmates. If you know all the words, continue to the Question Review.

brilliant	craters	ozone layer
clockwise	diameter	rotates
counterclockwise		

QUESTION REVIEW

Go back to the questions on pages 112 and 113. Look at your answers. Work with a partner. Look at your partner's answers too. Are they the same as your answers? Help each other write the correct answers.

PRE-READING 3

FOCUS QUESTION

Skim the reading on pages 116, 117, and 118 to find the answer to the question below. Underline the answer in your book. Write the answer below.

■ *Name the five outer planets in our solar system.* _____

_____

DETAIL QUESTIONS

Read "The Outer Planets" on pages 116, 117, and 118. Find the details. Underline the answers in your book. Write the answers below. As you read, write down on your vocabulary tickets any words you do not understand or cannot pronounce.

1. What is the name of the largest planet? _____

_____

2. What is the Great Red Spot on the surface of Jupiter? _____

_____

3. Give two reasons why some scientists say that Jupiter is a star

and not a planet. _____

_____

4. What is the name of the second largest planet? _____

_____

5. How long does it take Saturn to go around the sun? _____

_____

6. What are Saturn's rings made of? _____

_____

7. What are the names of the last three planets discovered?

_____

_____

The Outer Planets

Jupiter, Saturn, Uranus, Neptune, and Pluto are the planets farthest from the sun in our solar system.

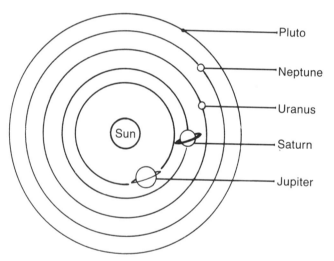

Jupiter is the largest planet in our solar system. Astronomers often use the word **jovian** to describe things on Jupiter. Jupiter is 484 million miles from the sun. The diameter of Jupiter is 87,000 miles, about 11 times greater than Earth's.

Jupiter is the fastest planet. It rotates very quickly. A day on Jupiter is only 9 hours and 50 minutes long. No other planet in our solar system spins so fast. It takes Jupiter 4,365 days to go around the sun.

Jupiter has 2.6 times the gravity of Earth. If you tried to jump on Jupiter it would be very hard. A person who weighs 100 pounds on Earth would weigh 260 pounds on Jupiter!

The atmosphere on Jupiter would not support life as we know it. There is no oxygen on the planet. The atmosphere contains other gases such as helium, hydrogen, methane, and ammonia. The gaseous formations in the atmosphere create dark and bright bands and a Great Red Spot on the surface. This Great Red Spot is most likely a huge storm on the planet's surface. Jupiter is surrounded by a ring and has 16 satellites.

Jupiter

Some scientists believe that Jupiter is not a planet but a star that has burned out. One reason they believe this is because Jupiter is a huge ball of gas. Another reason scientists believe Jupiter may have been a star is because it puts out more heat than it receives.

Saturn is the second largest planet in our solar system. A day on Saturn is 10 hours and 15 minutes. It takes Saturn 10,767.5 days to orbit the sun. Some scientists believe that Saturn is loosely packed snow

Saturn

and ice. If this is true, Saturn is the largest snowball ever! The atmosphere on Saturn contains hydrogen, methane, and ammonia. It will not support life as we know it.

The most unusual thing about Saturn is the system of rings. Saturn is often called the ringed planet. The rings of Saturn look solid, but they are not. The rings are made of **ice-coated** particles. These particles revolve around the planet like tiny satellites. In addition to the rings, Saturn has 23 satellites.

Uranus was discovered in 1781 by William Herschel. It is the third largest planet in our solar system. It has a diameter of 30,000 miles. It also has a system of rings around it like Saturn.

The discovery of Uranus led scientists to find two other planets. Shortly after the discovery of Uranus, astronomers began to notice that Uranus did not follow the path, or orbit, it should. They decided there must be an unknown object that was changing the orbit with its force of gravity. The planet Neptune was discovered in 1846.

Even after the discovery of Neptune and the corrections made for its gravity, the motion of Uranus was still considered strange. Finally in 1930, the planet Pluto was discovered. Pluto is the outermost planet in our solar system.

Uranus, Neptune, and Pluto are so far away from the sun that very little is known about them. Scientists are now learning new information about these distant planets from the **space probe** *Voyager I*. A space probe travels through space and collects information about the solar system. The space probe is sending information from outer space to the scientists back on Earth.

Besides the nine major planets in our solar system, there are thousands of minor planets called **asteroids**. Asteroids are small planets. The largest is called Ceres. It has a diameter of 665 miles. The smallest asteroid found so far is about .6 miles in diameter. These asteroids form a **belt** around the sun.

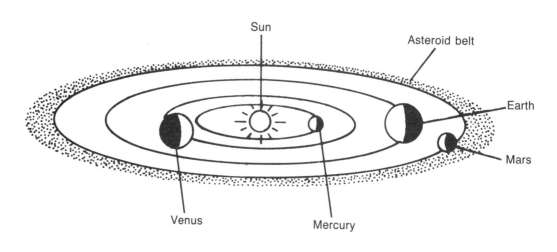

In this reading you learned some interesting facts about the outer planets in our solar system. You know that none of these planets has an atmosphere that could support life as we know it on Earth. Earth is the only planet in our solar system that can support human life.

SELF-EVALUATION 3

VOCABULARY TICKETS

Read the vocabulary tickets with your teacher and the whole class. Are there still some words you do not understand? Write these words in a notebook. With a partner, write some example sentences using these new words. Talk about the meaning of these words with your classmates.

VOCABULARY CHECK

Here are some important words from this reading. Do you understand all of these words? Circle the words you do not understand. Then find the words in the reading. Talk about the meaning of these words with your classmates. If you know all the words, continue to the Question Review.

asteroids	ice-coated	space probe
belt	jovian	

QUESTION REVIEW

Go back to the questions on pages 115 and 116. Look at your answers. Work with a partner. Look at your partner's answers too. Are they the same as your answers? Help each other write the correct answers.

CHAPTER REVIEW

Now that you have completed your reading about astronomy, go back to pages 107 and 108. Look at your first ideas about astronomy. Have your ideas changed? What have you learned? Talk about your ideas with the teacher and the whole class.

EXTENSION ACTIVITIES

A. THE SOLAR SYSTEM

Work with a group and make a picture of the solar system. Put in the sun, Earth, moon, the other planets, some additional satellites, and an asteroid belt. Add anything else that you think might be important. Try to remember the names of the planets, make them the right sizes and put them in their correct orbits around the sun. You may want to add color to your pictures.

B. MAKING CHOICES

Sit down in pairs or in groups of three. Use only one piece of paper. Match the words and phrases in Column A with the words and phrases in Column B.

Column A

_____ 1. Great Red Spot

_____ 2. supports human life

_____ 3. Earth's satellite

_____ 4. balls of gas

_____ 5. nearest star

_____ 6. *Voyager I*

_____ 7. red planet

_____ 8. ringed planet

_____ 9. evening and morning star

_____ 10. "We have just found another planet in our solar system."

_____ 11. a belt of minor planets

_____ 12. largest planet in our solar system

Column B

a. Saturn

b. William Herschel

c. Earth

d. asteroids

e. stars

f. a huge storm

g. a space probe

h. Mars

i. sun

j. Venus

k. Jupiter

l. the moon

GLOSSARY

asteroids Small, minor planets in our solar system.

astronomy The study of the planets and stars.

atmosphere A mixture of gases that surrounds the Earth or any other planet.

belt A band or strip around something.

brilliant Bright.

celestial body A planet, moon, star, or satellite in the sky.

clockwise The direction the hands move on a clock; to the right.

counterclockwise In the opposite direction that the hands on a clock move; to the left.

craters Large holes on the surface of a planet.

diameter A straight line passing through the center of a circle.

elliptical Having the form of an ellipse, or a curved, flattened circle.

ice-coated Covered with ice.

jovian An adjective describing things on Jupiter.

orbit A curved path that a celestial body takes around another celestial body.

ozone The layer in the atmosphere containing molecules with three oxygen atoms.

principal planets The nine planets in our solar system.

revolve To travel around; to orbit.

rotates Turns or spins.

satellites Celestial bodies orbiting planets.

solar system A group of planets and their satellites orbiting a star.

solar wind Movement of gases on the sun.

space probe An instrument or machine sent into space to collect information about the solar system.

stars Balls of gas that give off heat and light.

twinkle Rapid on-and-off light.